CHILDREN'S LITERATURE in an INTEGRATED CURRICULUM

THE AUTHENTIC VOICE

CHILDREN'S LITERATURE in an INTEGRATED CURRICULUM

THE AUTHENTIC VOICE

Bette Bosma and Nancy DeVries Guth
EDITORS

**International
Reading
Association**

**Teachers College
Columbia University
New York and London**

Published simultaneously by Teachers College Press, 1234 Amsterdam Avenue, New York, NY 10027 and The International Reading Association, 800 Barksdale Rd., Newark, DE 19714

Library of Congress Cataloging-in-Publication Data

Children's literature in an integrated curriculum : the authentic
　　voice / edited by Bette Bosma and Nancy DeVries Guth.
　　　　p.　　cm.
　　Includes bibliographical references and index.
　　ISBN 0-8077-3437-3 (pbk : alk. paper)
　　　1. Literature—Study and teaching—Case studies.
　　2. Interdisciplinary approach in education—Case studies.
　　I. Bosma, Bette, 1927–　　. II. Guth, Nancy DeVries.
　　LB1575.C55　　1995
　　372.64044—dc20　　　　　　　　　　　　　　　　95-11999

ISBN 0-8077-3437-3 (paper)
IRA Inventory Number 157

Printed on acid-free paper
Manufactured in the United States of America

02 01 00 99 98 97 96 95　　　8 7 6 5 4 3 2 1

Contents

Preface

Children's Literature in an Integrated Curriculum: The Authentic Voice emerged as a natural title for our book since for years we have been working together introducing teachers, parents, and students to books written by authors who speak with a true and authentic narrative voice. As the readers' involvement with such literature increases, so does their excitement for reading and learning. The enthusiasm of authors for their subjects is contagious. Curriculum becomes interesting and alive for students and teachers when taught through the deep feelings and perspectives of creative authors. Distance is removed and feelings, humor, and details are vividly etched in the mind of the reader.

At the present time, Nancy Guth, the reading/language arts supervisor in a growing school system in Virginia, serves the literacy concerns of administrators, teachers, paraprofessionals, specialists, and parents. She remains in frequent contact with her college mentor, Bette Bosma, who works on the cutting edge of reading/language arts theory to serve the needs of teacher education students at Calvin College in Grand Rapids, Michigan and teachers with whom she consults.

We could find no concise, workable guidebook to show teachers how to promote literacy by relating classroom curriculum to authentic literature. Quality children's literature is a natural bridge but busy teachers find it hard to find the time to collect and connect the literature. Nancy came to Michigan and persuaded Bette that teachers needed success stories. The teachers were eager to change their approach to their curriculum but wanted assurance that it would work. We began by brainstorming about exemplary classrooms that we had visited throughout the country and by inviting those teachers to share their success with us.

As we assembled the success stories of teachers using authentic literature within a connected curriculum, we were struck by the power of collaboration involved in each experience. In Chapter 1, we explain the theory that is foundational to a collaborative, integrated, literature-based curriculum. We use the definition of curriculum found in *Webster's New World Dictionary*: *all of the courses, collectively, offered in a school or in a particular subject.*

Each of the following chapters begins with an introduction written by either Bette Bosma or Nancy Guth (or both together) explaining how the chapter exemplifies the theory presented in Chapter 1. The accounts are grade-specific, but the content and concepts can be adapted to the developmental levels found in any grade. In Chapter 2, Marilyn Brower begins integration in two subjects and the beginning readers share their ventures in establishing a collaborative classroom. In Chapter 3, Jane Steffen Kolakowski elaborates on her use of the power of art to inspire all subjects in her collaborative second-grade classroom. In Chapter 4, we visit a middle school where Carole Geiger connects the curriculum and develops the art of language by engaging teachers and students with the power of quality picture books. In Chapter 5, Bette Bosma shares the power of a schoolwide focused study and explains how a large concept is developed into grade levels in a collaborative curriculum. In Chapter 6, Nancy Guth relates a success story of an at-risk student and describes how professional collaborations among a school specialist, supervisor, student, and classroom teacher accelerated his progress. In Chapter 7, Marilyn Thompson, Chapter One reading specialist, recounts collaborations in a multi-age school community with a broad overlying theme of gardening personalized by each level of learner. In Chapter 8, Norma Boehm describes how a small curriculum concept developed into a large collaborative classroom study, inspiring the teacher, student teacher, students, and parents. Chapter 9 ties together the experiences from a classroom teacher's point of view and the research/theory base of the university professor.

The children's books cited in the chapters appear at the end of each chapter, following the references. In some chapters, the list is further divided into topics or specific uses of the books. The purpose of this organization is to make it easier for busy teachers to assemble their own book collections.

Acknowledgments

We wish to express gratitude to the school administrators from Maine, Virginia, Michigan, and New Mexico, who encouraged their teachers to share their exemplary classrooms with us. A special word of thanks goes to the faculty of Rehoboth Christian School, New Mexico, who filled out lengthy questionnaires about their schoolwide study.

We are grateful to the children, teachers, and parents of Stafford County Public Schools, Virginia, for sharing their work and enthusiasm for collaborative curriculum.

We thank our husbands and our family members who took over household duties and who patiently endured our many hours on the computer and the telephone.

Finally, we thank Susan Liddicoat at Teachers College Press for her astute editing that helped us say what we meant to tell you.

CHAPTER 1

Making the Connections

Bette Bosma and Nancy DeVries Guth

More and more teachers are becoming excited about interrelating subject and skill within their classrooms. The excitement comes from seeing the students become enthusiastic, active learners within a classroom environment in which the teachers and students are partners in learning. Excitement also comes from seeing students becoming introduced to the personal voice of an author instead of the impersonal voice of a textbook. Other teachers are eager to try their hand at this rewarding way to teach but are unsure about how to begin and may feel overwhelmed, thinking that they must completely change what they have been doing. It is important to recognize that integration does not mean adding one more thing to an already crowded curriculum. Rather, it provides a different way of looking at what is already scheduled to be taught. This resembles a jigsaw puzzle in which the pieces are parts of the current curriculum that fit together to generate a complete picture. Each teacher's puzzle may be broken up differently, but the outcome will be true to the original goals and objectives.

The educators who wish to integrate curriculum are committed to a view of learning that sees all disciplines as interconnected and related to the life of the learner. They recognize that learning consists of searching for connections between the known and the new. It is an active process, rather than passive storage of isolated facts and skills. Our definition of integrated learning is the incorporating of language development and content, with emphasis on the interrelatedness of subject and skill areas, concepts and topics, within personal and shared contexts.

Teachers have found a natural beginning for integration of classroom subjects in children's literature, which complements each area of study. By means of quality literature, curriculum objectives can be gradually integrated throughout weekly plans. Literature provides real, purposeful reading. The practice of separating skill teaching from concept teaching

1

leaves children without the ability or motivation to connect new learning with what they already know. Students are often classified as *at risk* because they lack the ability to make connections between school learning and past knowledge. Books cross curriculum boundaries by offering a personal interpretation. They are the authentic voice that unites the curricular objectives.

In this chapter, we discuss the theory that connects curriculum, the possibilities for collaboration, the literature that helps connect learning, and the environment needed to accomplish this. In this book, we present success stories from teachers who have assembled their puzzle pieces in their own way. The result is a uniquely integrated curriculum that reflects the individual teacher's expertise and the students' interests.

THE CONNECTED CURRICULUM

Current demands for systematic change in education arise from recognizing the need for education to keep pace with today's complex global society. The teaching/learning component of systematic change is a shift from a traditional teacher-directed, content-based curriculum with separate disciplines to one that offers interdisciplinary studies characterized by active learning, shared decision making, and expectations of higher levels of achievement for all students (Anderson, 1993).

The concept of integrated curriculm is not new to the 1980s and 1990s. John Dewey (1938) proposed an integration of knowledge and experience; he recommended combining subject areas into theme studies and incorporating real-life activities into the classroom. Unfortunately, Dewey's ideal progressive classroom was often implemented unsuccessfully and accompanied by severe criticism. The Thorndike model of formal, content-based curriculum, including a fervor for accountability through formal testing, became dominant in the 1940s and 1950s and continues to prevail in many schools.

Throughout the past three decades, educational psychologists have offered theoretical support for planning curriculum with consideration for how children learn. When Piaget's and Vygotsky's works were translated into English, a renewed interest in child-centered teaching arose. Piaget emphasized providing a supportive learning environment to enhance children's cognitive development (Piaget & Inhelder, 1969). Vygotsky (1978) maintained that learning and development are interrelated from the child's first day of life and emphasized the importance of the social nature of human learning. Continued research in peer interaction, such as that of Forman and Cazden (1985), has influenced teachers to use the social classroom environment for effective learning.

Vygotsky (1978) sought a comprehensive approach to understanding the mind that would both describe and explain higher psychological processes. He did not achieve this goal, but the translation of his work has influenced research into brain functions from that day to the present time. Today, research affirms the complexity of the human brain and leads the educator to go beyond a narrow definition of learning. Curriculum planning should embrace the potential of the brain in searching for common patterns and relationships. Renate and Geoffrey Caine (1994) address this conclusion in *Making Connections: Teaching and the Human Brain*:

> Brain-based learning . . . rests on the fact that the various disciplines relate to each other and share common information that the brain can recognize and organize. This, for instance, is at the heart of thematic teaching.
>
> Because the learner is constantly searching for connections on many levels, educators need to orchestrate the experience from which learners extract understanding. They must do more than simply provide information or force the memorization of isolated facts and skills. (p. 5)

Our challenge is to stimulate the flow among the various subject areas as opposed to perpetuating a separate subject orientation. Figure 1.1 summarizes the differences between traditional and brain-based teaching as proposed by the Caines (1994).

Researchers offer a variety of basic principles to govern their concepts of integrated curriculum (Caine & Caine, 1994; Fogarty, 1991; Fogarty, Perkins, & Barell, 1992; Gardner, 1982). The principles advocating integrated curriculum that we follow in this book include the following:

1. The human brain has an infinite capacity to make connections. Common patterns facilitate information-processing strategies and the integration of sensory experiences. The Caines (1994) define brain-based learning as "learning [that] involves acknowledging the brain's rules for meaningful learning and organizing teaching with those rules in mind" (p. 4). The role of the teacher is to coordinate experiences from which the learners can make connections.

2. Education is concerned with meaningful knowledge, not surface knowledge. To make sense of the information received requires purposeful learning. A motto for our classrooms in the twenty-first century could be *Learning to think/ Thinking to learn*. It is not productive to pour into students' heads facts on nonrelated subjects and then expect them to pull out the facts on a test. Rote memory does not provide a sufficient measure of learning. Real learning requires personal connections.

3. An understanding of intelligence includes consideration of not only logical-mathematical and verbal abilities, but also musical, spatial, body-

FIGURE 1.1. Comparison of teaching models

Elements of Orchestration	Traditional Teaching	Brain-Based Teaching
Source of Information	Simple. Two-way, from teacher to book, worksheet, or film to student.	Complex. Social interactions, group discovery, individual search and reflection, role playing, integrated subject matter.
Classroom Organization	Linear. Individual work or teacher directed.	Complex. Thematic, integrative, cooperative, workstations, individualized projects.
Classroom Management	Hierarchical. Teacher controlled.	Complex. Designated status and responsibilities delegated to students and monitored by teacher.
Outcomes	Specified and convergent. Emphasis on memorized concepts, vocabulary, and skills.	Complex. Emphasis on reorganization of information in unique ways, with both predictable outcomes, divergent and convergent, increase in natural knowledge demonstrated through ability to use learned skills in variable contexts.

Source: *Making Connections: Teaching and the Human Brain* (p. 124) by R. M. Caine and G. Caine, 1994. Reprinted by permission.

kinesthetic, interpersonal, and intrapersonal intelligences (see Gardner, 1985). This in-depth understanding requires offering a wide variety of opportunities for active learning and recognizes that students will face a task or understand a concept through varying approaches.

  4. A literate classroom environment is an integral part of successful learning. Creating a classroom in which communication is of central importance is crucial to constructing meaning through language. In a language-rich environment, reading and writing are perceived as natural companions to speaking and listening and as natural outcomes of thinking. The

environment will be a place for relaxed conversations and dynamic stimulation, for trying out new ideas without fear of ridicule or labeling.

There are many models of integrated curriculum today. In practice, there is no one right model. By creating an environment in which learning activities require students to engage in all aspects of the language arts, an integrated curriculum is developed naturally.

COLLABORATION

The terms *teacher-centered* and *child-centered education* have been used frequently to describe different approaches to curriculum. A term surfacing more recently has been *collaborative curriculum*. This term is used to describe the best of both the teacher-centered approach, focused and directed by the teacher, and that of the child-centered approach, when curriculum is constructed around the interests and developmental abilities of each child. When teachers serve as both guides and participants in the classroom, their collaboration with students, with other teachers, with administrators, and with parents offers a synthesis for change. Lieberman (1992) suggests that collaboration is an important element of educational reform. She states:

> A growing body of research into new practices is helping us to understand that schools must develop collaborative, inquiring workplace environments for teachers at the same time that they are being developed for students. Many teachers involved in restructuring schools recognize the connection between their own development and the development of the students they teach; between their increased role in decision making and providing more choices for their students. Perhaps this obvious, yet elusive idea, provides the conceptual framework for the current reform movement. (p. 8)

School reform literature indicates that collaboratve work among peers changes the teachers' sense of community and increases their commitment to instructional innovations (Louis, 1992). The classroom teacher is working together with resource personnel, such as specialists in reading, speech, art, talented and gifted programs, and special education. The collaborative consultant role focuses on providing training and support for classroom teachers and promotes joint problem solving.

Teacher collaboration and continual professional inquiry into teaching and learning practices create new roles and relationships within school faculties and within the larger educational community. Teachers working together experience substantial improvements in student achievement as well as in behavior and attitudes (which often results in higher achievement as well). Parents notice their child's increased engagement with school and offer their own expertise and enthusiasm for school projects. Collaboration develops congruently with interpersonal relationships. When people reach out to offer ideas to one another, behavior becomes focused on sharing learning goals and teaching resources.

Many of the teachers described in this book began their puzzle solving alone in their schools and then learned that collaborating with others made the transition easier. Some teamed with university professors who were eager to observe how current educational theory works with real children. Others had the expertise of local specialists, such as language arts/reading personnel, special education teachers, or librarians/media specialists, to help them. Partnerships developed between teachers and student teachers and among other teachers at the same grade level. The teachers became more adept at shared planning with the students and developed stimulating collaborations within the classroom. Teacher–small group collaborations, peer partnerships, and peer groups led to a cooperative, collaborative milieu for the whole class.

The collaboration described in Chapter 5 involved all the teachers and the principal working together in a schoolwide study. In Chapter 7, a school applied for an early childhood grant to allow the entire school to develop its vision of collaboration. The collaboration began with the principal, teachers, and paraprofessionals, and soon extended to all the students. In the art study described in Chapter 3, parents, so intrigued by their second-graders' talk about Rembrandt, Mary Cassatt, and other great artists, were lured into the classroom—and stayed as volunteers and tour guides for field trips.

ROLE OF CHILDREN'S LITERATURE
IN AN INTEGRATED CURRICULUM

The curriculum connections that teachers make, and the personal connections that students make, provide a tapestry of meaningful knowledge. Children's literature holds an important place in this process. In weaving a tapestry, the warp, the thread running lengthwise in the loom, is the foundation or essence of the artistic piece. The woof, the horizontal threads, give the weaving its texture. If the subject area, topics, or concepts make up the warp of a tapestry of knowledge, children's literature offers the woof. The tapestry that is woven reflects the quality of the material used in the weaving: the better the book, the firmer the interconnectedness. It is possible to find children's literature that complements any curriculum. The quality literature becomes the thread that weaves curriculum objectives from one subject area or topic through other necessary components of the curriculum.

Literature provides the texture for joining the impersonal subject matter and the personal connections to be made by the student. Each genre makes a distinctive contribution. Poetry has a place in the classroom every day. Listening to "Arithmetic" by Carl Sandburg (1982) sets the stage for good-humored attention to mathematical figuring. Myra Cohn Livingston's *Sky Songs* (1984) and *Space Songs* (1988) explore the wonder of outer space and stimulate imaginative inquiry into the unknown. The paintings by Leonard Fisher in the Livingston poetry books add grandeur and beauty, and they have inspired many children to try their hand with a variety of media. Art appreciation and instruction begin with *Sing a Song of Popcorn*, poems selected by Beatrice de Regniers (1988) and illustrated by nine Caldecott Medal artists. A comparison of art styles and visual interpretations of the poetry widens the horizon for the budding child artist. *Were You a Wild Duck Where Would You Go?* by George Mendoza (1990) and *Animals, Animals* by Eric Carle (1989) deserve an integral part in an animal study for any age. Not only will the poetry and illustrations stimulate imagination; they will also prompt questions and comparisons. *All the Colors of the Race* by Arnold Adoff (1982) celebrates the cultural diversity of today's classrooms.

Well-written realistic fiction complements all subject areas and adds a personal dimension that makes learning memorable. The plot and setting connect with social studies, science, arithmetic, or the fine arts, while the underlying theme advances a psychological or philosophical reality that connects with the reader. *The Bee Tree* by Patricia Polacco (1993) combines a chase for honey with a recognition of the value of reading. The fascination of Ellen Raskin's *The Westing Game* (1978) lies in both the mathematical puzzles and the complexity of the human characters. *Shiloh* by Phyllis Naylor (1991) gives the reader both a realistic view of life in West Virginia and a sense of how complicated life becomes when keeping a secret.

Picture books are appealing to all ages and encompass all topics. Many lovely books feature accounts of places and events in the lives or memories of the authors. This realistic, yet fictional, look at a slice of life is especially effective in the geographical or historical dimension of a thematic unit. The voice of the people who lived in a specific time and place is captured by the authors. This voice combines with the well-researched illustrations to place the reader in an authentic historical setting. *Home Place*, told by Crescent Dragonwagon (1990), is stunningly illustrated by Jerry Pinkney. *Great-Grandma Tells of Threshing Day* by Verda Cross (1992) brings to life a midwest farm in the early 1900s. *My Grandmother's Journey* by John Cech (1991) tells fascinating tales and is colorfully illustrated by Sharon McGinley-Nally. In *The Keeping Quilt*, Patricia Polacco (1988) tells through pictures and words her story of a quilt that comes to America from Russia.

Historical fiction has long had a place in social studies, encompassing both history and geography. In addition, this genre offers many books that serve as models of language use, writing skill, and novel study. The personal voice of the author provides a more interesting medium through which students can become more involved in their study of history. When studying the westward expansion of the United States, students experience the frustration of the Donner family when they read *Patty Reed's Doll* (Laurgaard, 1989). They can identify with the orphan train children described by Joan Lowery Nixon (1988–1989). This quartet of books offers lively plots based on true stories of children sent to new homes in the West from New York City from 1854 to 1929. *Number the Stars* by Lois Lowry (1989) is an exciting story of the Danish Resistance in World War II. Ann Cameron's (1988) *The Most Beautiful Place in the World*, an account of growing up in the mountains of Guatemala, is a gem for all classrooms.

Traditional literature has a place in the classroom from kindergarten through high school. Myths, legends, fairy tales, and traditional animal tales should be interwoven in the tapestry of learning to provide an essential and imaginative basis of storytelling. They provide the cultural background so necessary for the diverse population of the United States and Canada. *Tales from Gold Mountain*, retold by Paul Yee (1989), gives Chinese Americans a sense of their past. John Steptoe's (1987) African version of Cinderella, *Mufaro's Beautiful Daughters*, gives African American children pride in their heritage. Native American explanations for the wonders of nature, such as those told in Michael Caduto and Joseph Bruchac's (1988) *Keepers of the Earth*, disclose the natural urge humans have to answer universal questions of identity. Specific ideas for using folk literature and a guide to recommended books for the classroom are found in Bosma (1992a).

A solid basis in traditional folk literature helps the more realistic child understand and appreciate modern fantasy. Modern fantasy writers borrow characters, motifs, and plots from folk literature. These modern tales present the child's world in a new perspective and help children understand their own world more clearly. Chris VanAllsburg's *Just A Dream* (1990) or Dr. Seuss *The Lorax* (1981) provide vivid imaginings of how life is affected if we don't take care of natural resources. *The Magic Schoolbus* books by Johanna Cole (1986–1992) enhance science and social studies with a fantastical interplay of real and imaginary happenings. Creative teachers will find that fantasy greatly enhances integrated studies and helps children visualize a variety of possible solutions to problems. In high fantasy, such as Madeleine L'Engle's *A Swiftly Tilting Planet* (1978) or Lloyd Alexander's *The Book of Three* (1964), the middle school student finds how important scientific understanding and general geographic knowledge is for the writer of fantasy.

The subsequent chapters in this book demonstrate how valuable nonfiction informational books and biography are in classrooms. The well-written informational book is much more than a source of knowledge. A book such as Peter and Connie Roop's *Seasons of the Cranes* (1989) arouses interest in the process of investigating wildlife and awe concerning the instincts of birds. Good nonfiction authors are writing about topics they enjoy, and their enthusiasm radiates throughout the pages. The personal voice of the author makes informational books an important influence in the classroom (Bosma, 1992b). Barbara Elleman (1992), editor of *Book-Links*, gives the following criteria for how good nonfiction authors approach their subject:

> The content should transport children to new horizons, provide diverse viewpoints on controversial matters, and discuss interrelationships between topics.
> Children should be taught early on that there are nearly always two sides to any issue or event, and opposing viewpoints should be introduced. They should also learn that rarely do events happen or people exist in vacuums and that connections between the two are essential. (p. 32)

Of all the books that engage the reader in a personal relationship with the author, biographies top the list. Past presidents become real people in books such as *Franklin Delano Roosevelt* by Russell Freedman (1990) and *Bully for You, Teddy Roosevelt!* by Jean Fritz (1991). Some picture book biographies zero in on just the part of life that made the person a hero. *Flight* by Robert Burleigh (1991) uses Charles Lindbergh's diary in a breathtaking account of his flight. Mike Wimmer's illustrations bring the reader right into the plane with Lindbergh. Collective biographies of persons notable in a particular field furnish a personal context in the discovery of information. Doris and Harold Faber (1991) include 25 biographical sketches in *Nature and the Environment: Great Lives*. The Fabers introduce the reader to important people in the field and show how ideas concerning the environment have changed over time.

The rest of the chapters in this book show how important a wide variety of children's literature is as children become more active in their own learning. Stimulating, exciting books become the catalyst for more reading, and both the teacher and librarian are challenged to provide enough books to satisfy the curiosity of eager students. Just providing the books is not enough. In planning integrated learning, a teacher must give careful consideration to building a learning environment. The language arts processes are thus taught in significant contexts with the necessary guidance for student understanding.

AN INTEGRATED CLASSROOM ENVIRONMENT

Teachers who are actively engaged in building a literary environment for their classrooms in which children can learn and will want to learn give constant attention to both the physical and the psychological aspects of learning. Successful implementation of an integrated curriculum requires an environment in which interactive learning can take place. The classroom must become a forum in which readers engage in congenial talk about books, authors, reading, and writing. An objective of such a learning environment is to create a space within which students can effectively engage in the literate behaviors of reading, writing, listening, speaking, thinking, and creating. The literary environment is not the end product, but the arena for developing thinkers and problem solvers who know how to learn and then apply this knowledge to each new experience.

When children enter a room in which desks are set row upon row facing a teacher's lecture area, they assume a passive mode. They are receivers, waiting for signals from the teacher before they engage in learning. By contrast, an interactive classroom will have desks or tables grouped for discussion, places for private work, and a whole-class meeting area where children gather to listen and talk spontaneously or at planned intervals. Where space is limited, this environment could be achieved through changeable seating arrangements, with the students taking the responsibility for moving furniture if necessary.

Everything in a classroom either contributes to learning or detracts from it. Nothing is neutral. Periodic inventories of the state of the room help the teacher focus on maintaining a creative learning environment. This requires careful attention to traffic patterns, lighting, noise reduction, and use of display space. The difference between a decorated room and a literate one includes involving the children in filling display spaces. Groups or individuals can share their learning with the class through bulletin boards reserved for their use. Colorful posters can remind the students of both their responsibilities and opportunities within the room. Including students in planning a careful use of all available storage space strengthens their ownership of the classroom. For example, we saw a third-grade classroom where large envelopes on a bulletin board named the current working groups. The teacher reported that her students store their working materials there and take the envelope with them to group meetings. Another teacher showed us bulletin boards that the students put up about their hobbies, families, interests, and travels. A bonus for her is the time she saves from tasks she used to do herself.

The teacher's concept of a learning environment influences how effectively the psychological needs for constructive learning are met. This requires a conscious effort to communicate that literacy is desirable and attainable by all. It requires self-examination of the teachers' attitudes, approach to learning, and goals for their students. It promotes the students' sense of ownership for both the process and content of their learning. It fosters a realization that the teacher is a partner in learning rather than simply the originator of topics and ideas. Most important, it provides a safe place where children dare to express themselves without ridicule or worrying that their answers will be wrong. Children and teachers together establish classroom behavioral guidelines and procedures. Tasks are clearly defined and needs are anticipated so that time and attention problems are kept to a minimum. The amount of effort that teachers expend at the beginning of the school year to build a literate environment contributes to an easier maintenance, especially if children capture the sense of ownership. When children become interested and involved in learning, behavior becomes focused on positive activity and classroom noise becomes the sound of learning rather than disruption.

Although the classroom accounts in the following chapters do not directly address building environment, the level of activity and involvement by the children reveal the quality of the learning environment that exists in each classroom. This does not occur without conscious efforts to ensure smoothly functioning classrooms.

REFERENCES

Anderson, B. L. (1993). The stages of systemic change. *Educational Leadership, 51*(1), 14–18.

Bosma, B. (1992a). *Fairy tales, fables, legends, and myths* (2nd ed.). New York: Teachers College Press.

Bosma, B. (1992b). The voice of learning: Teacher, child, and text. In E. B. Freeman & D. G. Person (Eds.), *Using nonfiction trade books in the elementary classroom: From ants to zeppelins* (pp. 46–54). Urbana, IL: National Council of Teachers of English.

Caine, R. M., & Caine, G. (1994). *Making connections: Teaching and the human brain.* Palo Alto, CA: Addison Wesley.

Dewey, J. (1938). *Experience and education.* New York: Macmillan.

Elleman, B. (1992). The nonfiction scene: What's happening? In E. B. Freeman & D. G. Person (Eds.), *Using nonfiction trade books in the elementary classroom: From ants to zeppelins* (pp. 26–33). Urbana, IL: National Council of Teachers of English.

Fogarty, R. (1991). *How to integrate the curricula.* Palatine, IL: IRI/Skylight Publishing.

Fogarty, R., Perkins, D., & Barell, J. (1992). *How to teach for transfer.* Palatine, IL: IRI/Skylight Publishing.

Forman, E. A., & Cazden, C. B. (1985). Exploring Vygotskian perspectives in education: The cognitive value of peer interaction. In J. Wertsch (Ed.), *Culture, communication, and cognition: Vygotskian perspectives* (pp. 323–347). New York: Cambridge University Press.

Gardner, H. (1982). *Art, mind and brain.* New York: Basic Books.

Gardner, H. (1985). *Frames of mind: The theory of multiple intelligences.* New York: Basic Books.

Lieberman, A. (Ed.). (1992). *The changing contexts of teaching: 91st yearbook of the National Society for the Study of Education.* Chicago: National Society.

Louis, K. S. (1992). Restructuring and the problem of teachers' work. In A. Lieberman (Ed.), *The changing contexts of teaching: 91st yearbook of the National Society for the Study of Education* (pp. 138–156). Chicago: National Society.

Piaget, J., & Inhelder, B. (1969). *The psychology of the child* (C. Gattegno & M. F. Hodgson, Trans.). New York: Basic Books.

Vygotsky, L. S. (1978). *Mind in society.* Cambridge, MA: Harvard University Press.

CHILDREN'S BOOKS

Adoff, Arnold. (1982). *All the colors of the race.* Illustrated by John Steptoe. New York: Lothrop, Lee & Shepard.

Alexander, Lloyd. (1964). *The book of three.* New York: Holt.

Burleigh, Robert. (1991). *Flight: The journey of Charles Lindbergh.* Illustrated by Mike Wimmer. New York: Philomel.

Caduto, Michael, & Bruchac, Joseph. (1988). *Keepers of the earth.* Illustrated by J. K. Fadden & C. Wood. Golden, CO: Fulcrum.

Cameron, Ann. (1988). *The most beautiful place in the world.* New York: Knopf.

Carle, Eric. (1989). *Animals, animals.* New York: Philomel.

Cech, John. (1991). *My grandmother's journey.* Illustrated by Sharon McGinley-Nally. New York: Bradbury.

Cole, Joanna. (1986). *The magic school bus at the waterworks.* Illustrated by Bruce Degen. New York: Scholastic.

Cole, Joanna. (1989). *The magic school bus inside the earth.* Illustrated by Bruce Degen. New York: Scholastic.

Cole, Joanna. (1990a). *The magic school bus inside the human body.* Illustrated by Bruce Degen. New York: Scholastic.

Cole, Joanna. (1990b). *The magic school bus lost in the solar system*. Illustrated by Bruce Degen. New York: Scholastic.

Cole, Joanna. (1992). *The magic school bus on the ocean floor*. Illustrated by Bruce Degen. New York: Scholastic.

Cross, Verda. (1992). *Great-grandma tells of threshing day*. Illustrated by Gail Owens. Morton Grove, IL: Albert Whitman.

deRegniers, Beatrice S. (1988). *Sing a song of popcorn*. New York: Scholastic.

Dragonwagon, Crescent. (1990). *Home place*. Illustrated by Jerry Pinkney. New York: Macmillan.

Faber, Doris, & Faber, Harold. (1991). *Nature and the environment: Great lives*. New York: Scribners.

Freedman, Russell. (1990). *Franklin Delano Roosevelt*. New York: Clarion Books.

Fritz, Jean. (1991). *Bully for you, Teddy Roosevelt!*. New York: Putnam.

Laurgaard, Rachel K. (1989). *Patty Reed's doll: The story of the Donner party*. Fairfield, CA: Tomato Enterprises.

L'Engle, Madeleine. (1978). *A swiftly tilting planet*. New York: Farrar, Straus & Giroux.

Livingston, Myra Cohn. (1984). *Sky songs*. Illustrated by Leonard Fisher. New York: Holiday House.

Livingston, Myra Cohn. (1988). *Space songs*. Illustrated by Leonard Fisher. New York: Holiday House.

Lowry, Lois. (1989). *Number the stars*. Boston: Houghton Mifflin.

Mendoza, George. (1990). *Were you a wild duck where would you go?* Illustrated by J. Osborn-Smith. New York: Stewart, Tabori & Chang.

Naylor, Phyllis. (1991). *Shiloh*. New York: Dell.

Nixon, Joan L. (1988a). *A family apart*. Book 1. New York: Bantam.

Nixon, Joan L. (1988b). *Caught in the act*. Book 2. New York: Bantam.

Nixon, Joan L. (1989a). *In the face of danger*. Book 3. New York: Bantam.

Nixon, Joan L. (1989b). *A place to belong*. Book 4. New York: Bantam.

Polacco, Patricia. (1988). *The keeping quilt*. New York: Simon & Schuster.

Polacco, Patricia. (1993). *The bee tree*. New York: Simon & Schuster.

Raskin, Ellen. (1978). *The Westing game*. New York: Dutton.

Roop, Peter, & Roop, Connie. (1989). *Seasons of the cranes*. New York: Walker.

Sandburg, Carl. (1982). *Rainbows are made*. Selected by L. B. Hopkins. San Diego, CA: Harcourt Brace Jovanovich.

Steptoe, John. (1987). *Mufaro's beautiful daughters*. New York: Lothrop, Lee & Shepard.

Seuss, Dr. [Theodor S. Geisel]. (1981). *The Lorax*. New York: Random House.

VanAllsburg, Chris. (1990). *Just a dream*. Boston: Houghton Mifflin.

Yee, Paul. (1989). *Tales from Gold Mountain*. Illustrated by Simon Ng. New York: Macmillan.

CHAPTER 2

A First-Grade Literature-Based Science Program

Bette Bosma and Marilyn Brower

This beginning excursion into integrated language development and science curriculum is offered to encourage teachers who are ready to try a shared curriculum but still feel tied to specific times for specific subjects. By starting with just two subjects, science and language arts, the partnership is a natural one for the learner and a manageable unit for the teacher. Time devoted to the study embraced the language arts and the science periods three days a week. The study soon connected with other subject areas because of the enthusiasm of the learners. In early childhood education, science centers on inquiry and discovery and focuses on the processes of questioning, reasoning, and using the scientific method for problem solving. Children's literature offers a source for answering the specific questions children ask and for stimulating further questioning. In the first-grade study described in this chapter, the variety of books the children heard and read nurtured their problem-solving skills and challenged their curiosity. In addition, the humor in the literature offered a light-hearted approach to the subject and engaged the interest of the less curious in the group.

This chapter grew out of a collaboration between a professor (Bette Bosma) and her graduate student. I (BB) was looking for a way to discover how children would respond to the exemplary nonfiction books I had collected and used in teacher education courses. Marilyn Brower, a first-grade teacher, agreed to use them at Jenison Christian School near Grand Rapids, Michigan, the school where she had been teaching. She was pursuing her master's degree in 1991, when the concept of integrating reading, language arts, and subject area teaching was taught in graduate courses but not always practiced in classrooms. For her master's project, she collaborated with a friend who was teaching first grade. Marilyn field-tested an integrated literature-based science curriculum, fitting her objectives into an existing curriculum based on *Accent on Science* (Sund, Adams, Hackett, & Moyer, 1983). The children's books she used appear with annotations at the end of the chapter. We also suggest sources for finding other current and appropriate books.

> Dear Animal Lovers,
> There were a lot of animals endangered in the book we read. We think it might be a good idea to build some cages to protect the bald eagle. We could protect the crocodile. We think that we should say that you can't hurt certain animals. We want to help the rhinoceros. We want to make sure that none of the animals get killed. We hope the monkeys won't die. Do you need money? We want to help.
>
> Sincerely yours,
> First-grade class
> Jenison, Michigan

The first-graders eagerly mailed their class letter to four organizations: the National Audubon Society, Greenpeace, the Humane Society, and the United States National Wildlife Federation. They also followed up with individual letters to these protective agencies.

One boy wrote to the National Audubon Society, "Sav the egle. Do you need mune?"

Another asked the National Wildlife Federation, "I love anmls. How cen I holp?"

The next day a child reported that he and his parents were going to plan a way to help endangered animals.

The fourth week of an active animal study found the children exhibiting a sense of power and planning additional science activities to satisfy their awakened curiosity. Basic concepts that carried through the various units of the science curriculum were observing, classifying, inferring, measuring, and predicting. A four-week animal unit included the concepts and vocabulary from the existing curriculum but did not confine the children's learning to the set curriculum. The animal study, formerly divided into Animals Around Us and Wild Animals, was divided into four parts: Pets, Farm Animals, Wild Animals, and Protected Animals and Zoo Animals. Lessons integrated science, music, art, reading, writing, speaking, and listening. Each lesson built on the former lesson and added a new element. The children and I (MB) together actively participated in the learning process, with the depth and direction of learning at times being controlled by the class or individual students. The plans followed the findings of Holdaway (1979), who indicated that encouragement of self-regulated learning in reading and writing for the young child is more beneficial to the learner than extrinsically applied instruction.

REPRESENTATIVE LESSONS

Four lessons are recounted in this chapter, one from each part of the animal unit, to demonstrate how the learning progressed. The books used in each lesson are described in an annotated bibliography at the end of the chapter.

Pets

The first lesson of the study on pets was based on the book *Guinea Pigs Don't Read Books* (Bare, 1985). The objectives of the lessons were for the children to identify various kinds of pets, to observe and describe characteristics of pets, and to record data on their own pet or a pet of their choice. The presentation of the lesson began with making a bar graph to record the children's pets. First the children's names were listed on the board with their pet or pets. Next a bar graph was constructed on a chart to show how many pets and what type of pets the children had (see Figure 2.1). The children all participated in counting up the various pets so the bar graph could be completed. They double-checked for accuracy and took turns filling in the bar graph.

A student's pet guinea pig was the special classroom guest for a week. She took center stage when the group read and discussed *Guinea Pigs Don't Read Books*. The children responded to both the photographs and the text, with the guinea pig owner and *About Animals* (Childcraft, 1989) used as sources for unanswered questions. The word *characteristics* was explained, along with charting information. Together the class constructed a chart with characteristics of a variety of pets (see Figure 2.2). The children used their prior knowledge gained from a previous science unit on the use of the five senses to describe the characteristics of each specific animal.

In response to the lesson, each student was responsible for at least one page in Our Class Pets information book. The children brought home their page and worked with their family members to complete it. On the back of their book page they drew a picture of themselves with their pet. Children with more than one pet could do a page for each pet if they wished. Those children without pets did a page on a favorite animal or an imaginary pet. Several children chose to do more than one page. One girl with no pets did three pages on pets she wished she had. A few children

FIGURE 2.1. Class pets graph

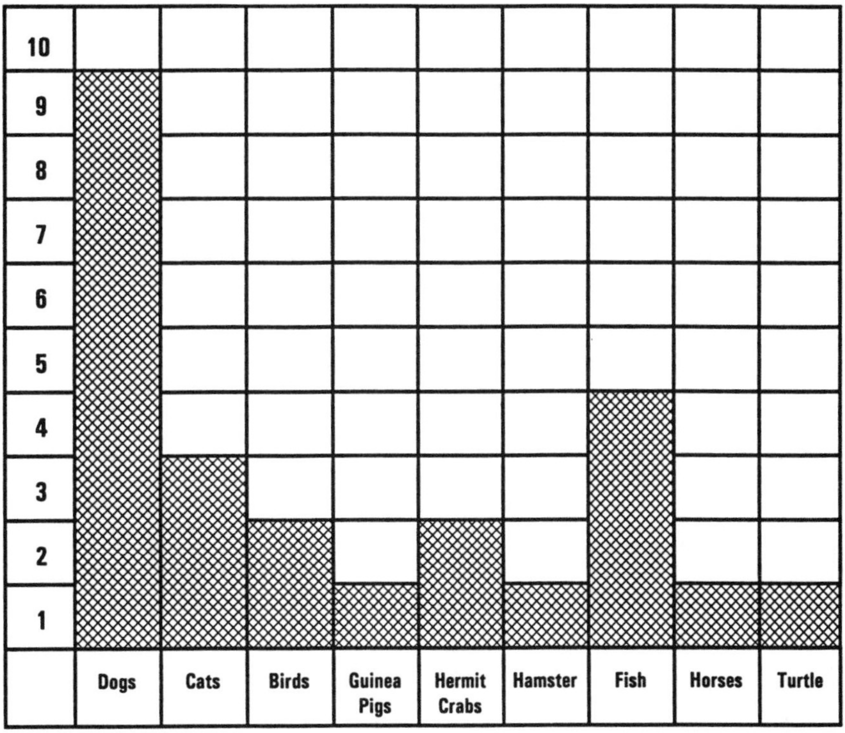

came back with incomplete pages with questions about how to do certain parts of their page. I worked with these students individually, getting information from the class chart, reference books, or their own background of information. Their pages were compiled into a book at the next meeting. The children delighted in reading the book aloud together.

The class book as well as the other two books used for this lesson were placed on a designated shelf. The children had opportunities during the day to read all of these books independently. The graph and chart made during this lesson were pinned on a large bulletin board simply titled "Animals." On four-inch colored construction paper circles, the children glued pictures of animals that were cut out from old magazines. Whenever possible the name of the animals was written in the circle, too.

Both the pupils and I enjoyed this lesson. The children were motivated throughout the lesson. I found that it was not necessary to pull any child along or back into the lesson. I also found that the investigation of

FIGURE 2.2. Pet characteristics chart

Animal	4 legs	2 legs	no legs	fur	feathers	shell	scales	tail	can run	can swim
dog	x			x				x	x	
cat	x			x				x	x	
bird		x			x			x		
guinea pig	x			x					x	
hermit crab							x		x	x
hamster	x			x				x	x	
fish			x				x	x		x
horse	x			x				x	x	
turtle	x					x		x		

the content was sparked by the book used. The continual oral exchange kept the children actively involved. They had a sense of responsibility for the lesson. They wanted to learn about pets and also to teach their classmates and teacher about their pet. The children began to see how to organize information through the use of charts and graphs. The importance of the written word was stressed throughout the lesson in a natural manner through the use of children's literature, graphs and charts, and then the children's own writing.

Farm Animals

The Farm Animals section began with a lesson on baby farm animals. Plans called for guiding the children to identify various farm animals, to describe uses of farm animals, to recall/predict/verify names of baby farm animals, and to describe how people care for farm animals. I began by recording on the chalkboard the names of animals that the children thought they would find on a farm. Since a wide variety of animals were listed, it was necessary to refine their definition of a farm animal. Through a lively interchange of ideas, prompted with an occasional clarifying question, the students narrowed the list to 15 animals they might find on a typical American farm. The first-graders' knowledge of farm animals was enhanced by their environment—the school is situated in a fast-growing community near Grand Rapids, Michigan, with some large dairy farms still operating in the area.

Next the children recalled or predicted names of these farm animals' babies. The children's responses soon filled the board next to each farm animal. The class listened intently to *Baby Farm Animals* (Windsor, 1984). The children responded throughout the reading with softly spoken "we were right," or "oops," if their predictions didn't match. Immediately after the story reading, the children suggested making a chart of the animals and their babies. They began proposing categories and quickly began designing the chart, putting to use their newly developed organization skills. They suggested two columns to include uses of farm animals and how people care for farm animals (see Figure 2.3). To the children's amazement, they had to leave many sections of the chart blank because they did not know the answers. Now they were eager to continue the search for information.

This was the fourth lesson taught in the field study. Dialogue among the classroom teacher, the children, and me (the teacher researcher), as well as among the children themselves, increased as they continued seeking, finding, and verifying needed information. The children would quickly refer to books in the classroom to verify their responses, often directing us to the exact page to confirm their response. At the conclusion of the charting activity I read a poem by Edith H. Newling, "The New Baby Calf" (Sutherland, 1976). Several children immediately requested a second reading. A prepared set of posters with a verse on each one made it possible for the children to join in on repeated readings. This was followed by each child working with a partner, illustrating a phrase of the poem. The class reassembled the now-illustrated poem and posted it on the wall. At the children's request, they read this poem together preceding each lesson on animals. Soon many children had memorized the poem and could be heard chanting it throughout the day.

Wild Animals

The third lesson of the week's study on wild animals was based primarily on the books *Wild Animals of Africa ABC* (Ryden, 1989) and *Tiger Trek*

FIGURE 2.3. Farm animals chart

Farm Animal	Baby Name	Uses of Farm Animals	How People Care for Farm Animals
cow	calf	milk	feed calf from bottle
horse	foal	round up cattle	ride to exercise them
hen	chick	eggs	clean pen
goat	kid		feed
pig	piglet	meat	spray to cool off
sheep	lamb		clip fur
cat	kitten	pet	give milk
turkey		food	
rabbit			
duck			
swan			
donkey			
dog			
pigeon			
goose			

Note: Chart completed with subsequent lessons.

(Lewin, 1990). Preceding lessons on wild animals helped children clarify their understanding of the differences between wild and domestic animals as well as learn about several different wild animals. The objectives of this set of lessons were to identify various wild animals of Africa, describe actions and characteristics of wild animals of Africa, and describe actions of the tiger.

The children found India on a map for a sense of the setting of this simple story about tigers. The hauntingly beautiful illustrations in *Tiger Trek* intrigued the children. Attention focused on the sequence of events during the second reading to model the structure of a prospective class-made book. Some children dictated while I wrote their sentences on individual tiger-shaped pages, while others wrote their own. Some children stuck close to the text, changing just a few words. They found the security they needed in the model of the book. Others expressed more creative or fanciful thoughts, showing readiness to move beyond the book. The children illustrated their tiger page using crayons and colored pencils. Then they initiated the sequencing of the story, with a minimum of guidance from me. They referred to *Tiger Trek* for ideas as they worked together to place their pages in order. The class book became a favorite to reread as a whole class, individually, and with a friend.

Protected Animals and Zoo Animals

The shift from a study of wild animals to protected, endangered animals was a natural one for the final week of study. The objectives of the first lesson were to identify various endangered animals, describe reasons for animals being endangered, list homeland and habitat of endangered animals, and extend the first-graders' vocabulary to include the words *endangered* and *extinct*.

The question written on the board preceding the reading of *Animals in Danger* (McCay, 1990) was simply "Why?" The lone word guided the children in their predictions as well as providing a purpose for the reading and viewing. The children gasped and oohed and ahhed as the first page of this book was opened and the animal in danger popped out. The pop-up book construction attracted the children's attention, but the simple, stark information kept them riveted. A large map near the reading circle furnished the sites where these eight endangered animals live. The clear text revealed the meaning of the new words, *endangered* and *extinct*.

"Let's make a chart," one of the children suggested. Charting was the favorite activity of most of the group. They agreed quickly on what to chart: animal name, homeland, habitat, reason for danger. Books used to complete the chart included *Animals in Danger* (McCay, 1990), *About Animals* (Childcraft, 1989), *The Vanishing Manatee* (Clark, 1990), and *Sea Otter Rescue* (R. Smith, 1990). The children initiated the discussion on human influence as the reason for danger for most of the animals. The children talked about other endangered animals known from their experiential background. Someone suggested that they write the four organizations named in the book, and a real-life writing experience began and was followed up by class members and their families.

The children moved on to comparing wild animals and those raised in captivity. *Gordy Gorilla at the San Diego Zoo* (Irvine, 1990) and *Orangutan* (Arnold, 1990) drew comparisons that the class discussed energetically with added questions and observations. *Zoo Animals* (Cortright, 1990) became their reference book when preparing for a field trip to the zoo.

CONCLUSIONS

The first-graders exhibited evidence of critical thinking as a result of the literature-based science lessons. Throughout the day the children talked about what happened in science and wrote about the science explorations in their journals. Science topics were chosen for self-selected creative writing. *Zoo Books*, a magazine previously displayed in the classroom but not chosen by readers, was now constantly being read. The excitement of the children and the depth of their science learning influenced the classroom teacher to extend the literature-based program to other units in the science curriculum. We found that children actively pursue their learning of content-area material when their literacy learning is encouraged and their total language development is broadened.

The use of children's literature in teaching content-area subjects such as science and social studies is a natural, integrated approach to teaching and learning. The personal voice of an enthusiastic author links the new information to realistic settings that even young children understand. This classroom action study was built on assumptions made by Weaver (1988), who found that children's conceptual background is broadened and increased motivation in reading and learning occurs with use of a variety of books. Informational books provided depth and richness of detail. They introduced the topic of study, provided the factual content, or became vital sources of additional information. By using several informational books on a single topic, different perspectives were explored (Kobrin, 1988). Making comparisons taught children to investigate different ideas and topics rather than blindly accept the author's attitudes and perspective. This encouraged children to ask themselves questions and make critical judgments about what they were reading. The critical comparison of books led to clearer thinking when children charted similarities and differences.

REFERENCES

Holdaway, D. (1979). *The foundations of literacy.* Sydney, Australia: Ashton Scholastic.

Huck, C.S., Hepler, S., & Hickman, J. (1993). *Children's literature in the elementary school* (5th ed.). New York: Harcourt, Brace, Jovanovich.

Kobrin, B. (1988). *Eyeopeners!* New York: Penguin.

Sund, R. B., Adams, D. K., Hackett, J. K., & Moyer, R. J. (1983). *Accent on science* (A Merrill Science Program). Columbus, OH: Merrill.

Weaver, C. (1988). *Reading process and practice.* Portsmouth, ME: Heinemann.

ANNOTATED BIBLIOGRAPHY
OF CHILDREN'S BOOKS FOR ANIMAL STUDY

The following bibliography includes all the books used in the first-grade study, not only the ones described in this chapter. If the particular books in this list are not available, you may be able to find similar books in school and public libraries that fit the suggested integration areas. The annual list of recommended books from the Orbis Pictus committee of the National Council of Teachers of English and the annual selection of "Outstanding Science Trade Books for Children" by a committee from the National Science Teachers Association and Children's Book Council are valuable references for book selection. Both are available from the sponsoring organizations.

Arnold, C. (1990). *Orangutan*. Photographs by Richard Hewitt. New York: Morrow Junior Books.
> Large photographs and detailed text help the learner gain much information on the orangutan. There are comparisons made between wild and domestic animals, animals in the wild and in captivity, and gorillas and chimps. Geography and history are naturally encountered in this book. It is above the first-grade level but is easily adapted for usage with young children.

Banks, Merry. (1990). *Animals of the night*. Illustrated by Ronald Himler. New York: Charles Scribner.
> Beautiful watercolor illustrations draw the reader into this simple story. The story contrasts humans retiring for the night and certain animals being active in the night. Tidbits of information are given on a variety of animals, enticing the reader to learn more about them.

Bare, Colleen S. (1985). *Guinea pigs don't read books*. New York: Dodd, Mead.
> A simple text reveals to the reader many things that guinea pigs can't do. This encourages the reader to think of things that guinea pigs *can* do, as well as learn more about this pet. The book could be used as a model to write a story about the child's own pet.

Barrett, Judi. (1970). *Animals should definitely not wear clothing*. Illustrated by Ron Barrett. New York: Atheneum.
> This easy-to-read book humorously illustrates a variety of animals in clothing. Several animals are pictured, and the first-graders wanted to draw and write about an animal in human clothing.

Carle, Eric. (1987). *Have you seen my cat?* New York: Franklin Watts.
> This beautifully illustrated book lends itself to a comparison of wild and domestic animals. The children discussed similarities and differences of a variety of cats.

Childcraft. (1989). *The How and Why Library: Vol. 5. About animals*. Chicago: World Book.
> Volume 5 is an excellent reference tool to be used in the classroom. The

children enjoyed seeking specific information as well as listening to interesting sections just for enjoyment.

Clark, Margaret Goff. (1990). *The vanishing manatee*. New York: Dutton.
This fascinating mammal is introduced thoroughly to the reader. The prose
style and content of this book would be best used with the upper elementary child. However, portions can be adapted for the younger child by providing explanations of terms or paraphrasing parts of it. Comparisons with
other sea creatures will occur naturally if time is allowed for children to respond.

Cortright, Sandy. (1990). *Zoo animals*. New York: Barrons.
This excellent reference book would offer a thorough preview before visit
to a zoo. Categories of information about each animal includes their home,
life span, appearance, babies, food, and habitats.

Hoban, Tana. (1985). *A children's zoo*. New York: Greenwillow.
Three adjectives describe each animal presented in this book. The simple text
and large pictures fit a young reader's interest. The writing style offers a
natural model for writing descriptive words on a variety of animals.

Irvine, Georgeanne. (1990). *Gordy gorilla at the San Diego zoo*. New York: Simon &
Schuster.
Beautiful photographs accompany the story and chronologically illustrate
the life of a young gorilla. Wild animals raised in the wild are compared to
wild animals raised in captivity. Also, the topic of endangered animals is explored.

Isenbart, Hans-Heinrich. (1981). *Baby animals on the farm*. Photographs by Ruth
Rau. New York: Putnam.
Fifteen farm animals are introduced in this book. The text is accompanied
by beautiful, large photographs of the animals with their babies. Information given on each farm animal is enough to entice the reader to learn more
about them from other classroom sources.

Keats, Ezra Jack. (1972). *Pet show*. New York: Macmillan.
A simple story is told of a city neighborhood pet show. Unfortunately, Archie
could not find his cat. All the other kids brought their pets and received rib-
bons for them. Archie resorted to bringing a germ in a jar, which won a rib-
bon for being the quietest pet at the show. Descriptive labels used in this
story model a creative writing activity using adjectives.

Lavies, Bianca. (1990). *The secretive timber rattlesnake*. New York: Dutton.
Beautiful, large photographs accompany a text that is written in a simple
and direct style. Especially interesting to the first-graders was the page on
the snake killing and eating a mouse. Much information is given on the timber
rattlesnake. It encouraged the children to learn about other reptiles.

Lewin, Ted. (1990). *Tiger trek*. New York: Macmillan.
Hauntingly beautiful illustrations accompany this simple story of a tiger trek.
Several other animals are introduced in relation to the tiger. The children
wanted to know more about these unique animals. The geographic location
is explored clearly.

McCay, William. (1990). *Animals in danger*. Illustrated by Wayne Ford. New York: Macmillan.

> Eight animals that are endangered are introduced in this book. The pop-up construction immediately entices the young reader to learn more about each animal. The animals' vanishing habitat and geographic location are of great interest to the reader.

McFarland, Cynthia. (1990). *Cows in the parlor: A visit to a dairy farm*. New York: Atheneum.

> The text of this book is simple. It describes life on a dairy farm as well as introducing its readers to dairy cows. Large photographs fit well with the text in portraying life on a dairy farm. This book led to a discussion comparing wild and domestic animals.

Paladino, Catherine. (1991). *Our vanishing farm animals: Saving America's rare breeds*. Boston: Little, Brown.

> The history and status of seven endangered farm animals are explored in this book. Large, detailed photographs accompany the simple text. The content is easily adaptable to several grade levels. This book could be used while studying either farm animals or endangered animals.

Parson, Alexandra. (1990). *Amazing birds*. Photographs by Jerry Young. New York: Knopf.

> Both large and small photographs illustrate the information given in short paragraphs. A wide variety of birds are introduced. This is an excellent handbook of information for the young reader.

Parsons, Alexandra. (1990). *Amazing mammals*. Photographs by Jerry Young. New York: Knopf.

> Many mammals are introduced to the reader in this book. A wide variety of photographs accompany the simple text. This book could be used as a reference tool or as an enjoyable information book to be read independently.

Parsons, Alexandra. (1990). *Amazing snakes*. Photographs by Jerry Young. New York: Knopf.

> Children of many ages enjoy this book of facts about snakes. The photographs encourage an emotional response from the reader. A lot of information is given in small paragraphs, which led to further exploration by one eager student.

Rambo, Dottie. (1981). *Down by the creek bank*. Nashville: Impact Records.

> This delightful song relays the tender connection between a child and an invisible dog. The wild antics of a pretend pet delighted the first-graders as they sang along with the record.

Ryden, Hope. (1989). *Wild animals of Africa ABC*. New York: Dutton.

> For each letter of the alphabet, a large photograph of a wild African animals is shown. Some of the animals are well known and others are relatively unknown. The book concludes with a brief paragraph of information on each animal. The unique and interesting bits of information intrigued the first-graders and would be appropriate for older children as well.

Smith, Roland. (1990). *Sea otter rescue: The aftermath of an oil spill*. New York: Dutton.
This book details humans' disastrous effect on a wild animal. Comparisons to other sea creatures are made, as well as comparisons to other animals adversely affected by humans. The content is generally geared to older children; however, portions could be adapted for young children.

Smith, Trevor. (1990). *Amazing lizards*. Photographs by Jerry Young. New York: Knopf.
The children were immediately drawn to this book on lizards. A lot of information is given in the text. The photographs enticed the young readers to learn about these unique and sometimes grotesque creatures.

Sutherland, Zena. (1976). *The Arbuthnot anthology of children's literature* (4th ed.). New York: Morrow.
This excellent resource offers a wealth of classic children's literature. The organization of the book helps you find a special, unique work that may fit a particular subject.

Windsor, Merrill. (1984). *Baby farm animals*. Washington, DC: National Geographic Society.
Life on a variety of farms is detailed in this book. Large photographs show many farm animals with their babies. The children were immediately drawn into this delightful book, which encourages further exploration of farms as well as farm animals and their babies.

CHAPTER 3

Reading and Rembrandt

An Integrated Study of Artists and Their Works

Jane Steffen Kolakowski

Memories—creating memories is the essence of reading instruction, instruction that causes students to learn interesting, informative information as well as developing their skills as strategic, fluent readers. Such is the theme of reading with the great artists, designed out of a passion for the art of great ones and a passion for teaching to the soul as well as the mind of second-grade students. Jane Kolakowski's students are not gifted. They are a heterogeneous group of second-graders from a school where almost half of the students qualify for free lunch. Some of the students live at the local homeless shelter, some at a local motel. Many of her students qualify for special education services, and others for Chapter One reading. However, after a year in Jane's room, any of her students would qualify for our gifted program on the basis of what is in their second-grade portfolio. Jane teaches each child as if he or she is gifted, and they all rise to her expectations. She does not teach; she creates learning memories for each of her students and guides them as they construct their personal search for meaning and connections.

As Eloise Greenfield (1993) points out:

> People are a part of their time. They are affected, during the time they live, by the things that happen in their world. Big things and small things. A war, an invention such as radio or television, a birthday party, a kiss. All of these experiences help to shape people, and they, in turn, help to shape the present and the future.

Connecting classroom concept areas develop naturally as literacy experiences are cultivated in the rich environment of Jane's classroom.

During the study described in the following chapter, her room resembles the National Gallery of Art, as well as the Library of Congress. She has extensively researched brain-based teaching and the relationship of the arts to learning. This research is illustrated in the way she teaches as well as by the materials she enticingly places all around the room. The literacy of the home is honored in the way she encourages contributions from all homes—artifacts, prints, and assistance. Her room is truly a community of learners, as student teachers, parents, school paraprofessionals, the reading specialist, the librarian, even school board members can be found daily collaborating with the children. Connections are discovered in every book read, every newspaper or magazine brought to school, and every speaker invited to the classroom.

She develops her classroom as a connection of her literate home, and her classroom illustrates the relaxed alertness described by Caine and Caine (1994) as the optimal state for learning. Students research their own hypothesis and celebrate their differences by excelling in their favorite areas while working to develop their challenges. Literature and language, mathematics and science, geography and multicultural awareness are blended so naturally that one ceases to be aware of each as a separate entity. At the end of the study, teachers as well as students were amazed by the amount of subject-area objectives naturally learned in the course of this memorable artistic journey.

After discussing and exploring the painting "Stafford Heights" by Gari Melchers, I asked my second-graders to imagine that they could enter the painting. Giovanni Baez wrote:

> I smell grain in the field. Not that many houses are around. Thare are many trees. It is sunny and thare is a dirt path. Thare's a field on a hill. It is bright outside the air is sweet the trees smell lik pinecones. Thare are no flowers here. My mouth waters when I tast sweet graps. You can not hear the birds singging. You can feel a breeze. You can't see anyone outside. The wind plays tug-o-war with my hair.

For me, her last sentence is perhaps the most beautiful metaphor I've ever read. What caused this sudden insight and maturity in such a young person? Can it be replicated with other students? I began a search to try to answer these questions.

Art education advocate Elliot Eisner (1981) contends that the arts offer a dimension to cognition that no other subject can. He points out that learning is a sensory experience. Therefore it makes sense that we should be helping students develop and refine their senses. This, Eisner says, is the role of the arts.

My own experiences in art galleries have shown consistent parallels between painting and story elements. I saw portraits and imagined them as characters. Landscapes were story settings. Genre paintings featured plot. I began to introduce these story elements through paintings, and the students became excited! In a short time, this language arts unit exploded into a totally integrated study and is now the most popular study of the year for my students.

My school is representative of the changing traditional school. Only five to eight years ago, it was an affluent country school. Now over 40% of the students receive a free lunch. Many students have had little literacy exposure prior to coming to school. A growing welfare and English-as-a-second-language population offers new challenges in the classrooms. However, this integrated study bridges the cultural and economic differences between students. It is a study that all lack background knowledge in, and therefore students enter from relatively the same place. And, more important, it is a study that celebrates the uniqueness of individuals.

COLLABORATION: THE ART OF LANGUAGE

Mike Venezia's (1990–1992) Getting to Know the World's Greatest Artists is a series of picture biographies that I use as the main sources and reading books for this study. Since the second-grade social studies curriculum in our county features Europe and America, I focus on European and American artists in this study. The students browse through the biographies before beginning the study and list their first, second, and third choices for the artist they would like to become a specialist about. Popular choices include da Vinci, Michelangelo, van Gogh, Mary Cassatt, Rembrandt, Picasso, and Edward Hopper. Using their choice indications, I group the children in groups of three to focus on a particular artist. Each group is responsible for creating a classroom bulletin board to teach others about their artist. (If I lack bulletin board space, I purchase project display boards for students to use. These are mobile and reusable.) The Venezia books and art prints (personally collected and borrowed from the art teacher) become core sources of information. If art prints are unavailable, children make their own by recreating some of the paintings found in the Venezia books.

Teacher-guided lessons are provided to the entire class about each artist, so everyone is exposed to them all. I like to use a storytelling approach. I read about the life of the painter ahead of time and share what I've learned with the class. We maintain a large chart divided into columns for each artist. As an artist is studied, students state pertinent information about the artist, and then I record it on the chart for easy reference. As the chart grows, comparing and contrasting of artists occurs as well as storytelling of special events in the lives of the painters. In addition, children learn to identify causes and effects in each artist's life.

Writing activities include working with descriptions in order to paint a picture of a favored artwork in words. Artist fact sheets similar to the wall chart are created, listing pertinent biographical data. Questions and statements are reviewed as students list questions they would like to ask and information they would like to tell the artist. Meghann Sokolowski's account shows her careful observation of "A Polish Nobleman" by Rembrandt:

> The Nobleman is dark. He seems to be glancing at somthing. He is wearing a fur coat and hat. He has a white earring shaped as a teardrop. He has a long curly mustach, and lots of glimering strings of gold. Thay are very shiny. He has a big pole, with sort of a cylender shaped plate of gold on the top. He is sort of old.

I have found the teaching of story elements a natural extension of painting. Landscapes are visual story settings. In addition to displaying a place, the time, and the weather, landscapes allow the imagination to wonder what sounds might be occurring and what scents might be smelled. Lively discussions ensue. Portraits invite talk of characterization. Who was this person? Can the students create a life for the individual? What book characters might the portrait be compared to? Genre paintings (those that feature action) present opportunities to discuss plot and dialogue. Students pose as the characters in the painting and create the dialogue and actions that might occur.

My students enjoy listening to fictional stories such as *Rembrandt Takes a Walk* (Strand, 1986), *Emma* (Kesselman, 1980), *Cathedral Mouse* (Chorao, 1988), *Matthew's Dream* (Lionni, 1991), *Appelemando's Dreams* (Polacco, 1991), *The Incredible Painting of Felix Clousseau* (Agee, 1988), and *Bonjour, Mr. Satie* (dePaola, 1991). But the favorite book has always been *The Girl with a Watering Can* (Zadrzynska, 1990) in which a young girl leaves her Renoir painting and wanders through the National Gallery of Art in Washington, D.C., creating havoc as she goes. For us in Virginia, a field trip to the National Gallery of Art is a natural follow-up to this study.

THE ARTISTIC JOURNEY

Since this study focuses primarily on European artists, the map of Europe becomes an important focus. I distribute a blank map of Europe (containing only the outlines of the countries) to each child. As an artist is studied, that artist's hometown is marked and labeled by the children on their map. Countries such as Italy, France, Spain, Germany, and the Netherlands become familiar. So do cities such as Paris, Rome, and Florence. For most second-graders, these geographic places are new to them. When locating these places on a globe or world map, a natural extension question is, "Where do we live?" Thus these new places are learned in relation to our U.S. home. Directional terms of north, south, east, and west become part of the vocabulary as places are discussed in relationship to each other. Games can be developed to practice this new knowledge, such as these riddle questions:

- I am the country north of Spain. Who am I?
- I am the sea that washes southern Europe. Who am I? What countries do I border?
- I traveled from Rome to Florence, Italy. Which direction did I go?
- I am lost. How can I get from Germany to Spain?

An in-depth study of one or more of the countries is also included. I have found that Italy works well, since Botticelli, da Vinci, and Michelangelo are Italians featured in the Venezia biography series and much additional information is available on them. These men lived during the Renaissance with its wonderful stories of intrigue and awakening of creativity and learning. Any encyclopedia can point the teacher and students to others of this era. France is another natural possibility, since many outstanding painters have strong ties to France, such as Monet, van Gogh, Mary Cassatt, Gauguin, and Picasso. Natural geography, customs, and holidays the painters may have enjoyed, as well as the country's flag and currency, can be explored. Simple phrases in the native language of the country and foods of that land are also taught.

THE ART IN MATHEMATICS

Money counting seems to be one of those difficult hurdles for primary grade students. In an attempt to motivate students to want to count money, I decided to create a situation reminiscent of real life—the art auction.

Throughout the year, I purchase six or eight postcards of paintings (art galleries have an abundance) that become the artworks for sale in the art auction. Other sources for free or low-cost art reproductions include calendars, magazines, and notecards. I watch for reproductions and do not confine them to works by painters studied. Introducing other artists and artforms expands the students' knowledge and leads them to self-discoveries.

To reinforce mathematics learning, I explain to the children that each center and activity in the classroom contains a monetary value. If the student completes that center/activity satisfactorily, he or she will be paid that amount in play money (paper currency is used for ease of handling). I teach daily lessons in money counting as a support to the center/activity work earnings. The skills learned in counting with the $1, $5, and $10 amounts transfer to counting with coins also.

Each activity carries a different value depending on the amount of work involved. As students work through their choice of centers and activities, they acquire money that they will keep in anticipation of our art auction. A paper wallet is given to each child to store this money in. (The wallet can be as simple as a sheet of construction paper folded in half and stapled on the two outer edges, forming a pocket for the bills.) The money earned becomes the amount each child will have to use at the art auction.

Typical centers/activities include:

- Reading a map ($25)—A riddle worksheet requires children to use their knowledge of directional terms to locate places in Europe
- Making a flag ($10)—Each child makes a construction paper flag of a European country
- Recreating a famous painting ($15)
- Scavenger hunt ($10)—Searching for particular items from the gallery of paintings in the classroom, players list the painter's name and painting title when it is found
- Reading and discussing with the teacher a book from the classroom enrichment library ($25)—These are fiction and nonfiction books set in a special place that pertain to the unit topic
- Completing an art word search ($5)
- Creating an art word search ($10)
- Writing a poem/story/biography about the "Mona Lisa" ($20)
- Writing a description of a painting in the classroom and seeing if the teacher can identify it ($25 if she can; $20 if she can't)—Good descriptions make clear to the reader what is being described
- Creating an original work of art that should hang in an art gallery some day! (Sell it to someone in the classroom for play money)
- Making a puppet of a painter and having it tell the class about its life ($20)

To help manage and keep a record of what each child has completed, I list all activities and centers with their amounts on paper and make copies for the children. On finishing an activity, the child brings the completed product and activity sheet to me. This allows for immediate feedback to the child, and money payment is made at this time. In addition, I can check that activity off on the sheet and write any anecdotal comments I wish to remember on the sheet. The collected sheets become a record of what each child accomplished as well as a source for anecdotal assessment. I make sure I set aside a time each day when I am available for students to present their completed work for this important feedback. I use this time to reinforce, encourage, and/or review with each child on his or her own level.

As the study proceeds, I am always intrigued to see how often the children take their earnings out of their wallets and count the money. Frequently they encourage each other to count by asking, "How much have you earned so far?" Peer tutoring occurs naturally as one child asks another, "Will you help me count my money?"

The math study culminates with an art auction. Upper grades may want to obtain the services of a real auctioneer. However, I have found that a guest in the classroom often puts pressure on second-graders. An auctioneer may be unfamiliar with youngsters and moves too quickly for them, causing frustration for all involved. A familiar face, such as the principal, is a more appropriate auctioneer for this age. I have assumed the role as well. I discuss bidding before the auction begins and provide several sessions of practice bidding. I also like to talk about sportsmanship before beginning. With only six to eight artworks to be auctioned, most children will not receive anything. I explain this to them ahead of time and explain that this is how it is at a real art auction, too. I want to make sure that children do not equate losing out to another with being a loser. This is an important life lesson. Learning about art and the pleasure of the contest should be explained as important benefits that all will win. Once these ground rules are established, the auction has always proceeded smoothly, albeit with much laughter and *much* money counting.

ART FROM ALL CULTURES AND AGES

An awareness of individuals' potential for great things is an underlying value that this study presents. To internalize this, children must be presented with examples from all cultures and ages, as well as all professions and walks of life. Throughout the school year, I continue to introduce my students to people from the arts who are from a variety of backgrounds other than European and a variety of ages other than mid-life adults.

Grandma Moses began her popular career in her late 70s. She was 100 years old when she painted the illustrations for a version of Clement C. Moore's poem, "A Visit from Saint Nicholas" (Biracree, 1989). Today the book is titled *The Grandma Moses Night Before Christmas* (C. C. Moore, 1991).

Native Americans can be supported through paintings. George Catlin was a nineteenth-century painter who tried to capture the ways of the Plains Indians through his artwork. His portraits are filled with possibilities for character study and writing opportunities. For Native American artists of today, an excellent source is *Native Artists of North America* (R. Moore, 1993). It is a book that presents Native American artists to young children and offers activities for children to try.

African American painter William H. Johnson (1901–1970) is presented in the book *Li'l Sis and Uncle Willie* (Everett, 1991). The illustrations are actual paintings of Johnson's in the collection of the National Museum of American Art, Smithsonian Institute. The story is based on actual events in his life.

Mexican Diego Rivera was a muralist whose wife, Frieda Kahlo, was also a distinguished painter. The biography of Rivera written by Jim Hargrove (1990) is written for older children and is an excellent teacher source for facts about this pair of artists. A Weekend with the Artist Series, published by Rizzoli International Publications, includes *A Weekend with Diego Rivera* (1994), narrated in the first person by the artist.

Teachers may know of African American Faith Ringgold as the author/illustrator of the award-winning book, *Tar Beach* (1991). A former teacher, she has also written and illustrated *Aunt Harriet's Underground Railroad in the Sky* (1992), a recounting of slavery and facts about Harriet Tubman's life. In addition, many teachers and students are fascinated by her studio art as well. In *Dinner at Aunt Connie's House* (Ringgold, 1993), Aunt Connie is an artist. The portraits on her walls speak. Each portrait is an African American who describes his or her contribution while cousins Melody and Lonnie listen, learn, and dream of their own future. This is a book to inspire students and teachers in the collaborative possibilities between the arts of reading, writing, painting, and the power of personal dreams. Faith Ringgold's studio art offers the same message. She is known for her storytelling textiles.

One of the painters featured in *Dinner at Aunt Connie's House* is Jacob Lawrence. Like Ringgold, Lawrence is an artist who has joined the children's literature community. His book *Harriet and the Promised Land* (1968/1993) is the story of Harriet Tubman. He combines poetry and painting to re-create a powerful story.

The artist possibilities for multicultural study are endless. Local art teachers and the art section in the public library can offer additional information.

FEEDBACK AND FOLLOW-UP

Parent response to the study has been wonderful. Unsolicited comments come back to me each year, and they have always been positive. Parent chaperones learn from the children as they stand together before a painting on our field trip to the National Gallery of Art. As siblings follow older sisters or brothers into my class, parents often ask if I am still teaching the unit and if they can chaperone the art field trip.

Students are the true test. Although the study began as an attempt to develop and refine the visual senses of my students as well as extend their understanding of story elements, a much greater and more subtle result always occurs. The students *do* learn to look more selectively, as is evidenced in their writings. But more happens as well. The study generates much enthusiasm in children as they discover the human qualities of painting. The topic feels safe to children who may not be comfortable taking risks; much of art is personal interpretation, which allows each to safely risk an opinion without fear of being mistaken. In addition, the people who created the paintings have stories and lives that fascinate this age group. A whole new world is opened, a world that shows students that possibilities exist within people. Ordinary people can do extraordinary things! Children start to dream about their own future and wonder about their own talents.

This study verifies for me the research of Elliot Eisner (1992) in which he writes that the arts' contribution is its offer to everyone of an ability to feel and participate in the lives of others. Art is communication with oneself and with others. Art unites the rational and the emotional. Plato spoke of the differences between the heart and the head but felt they both had contributions to make to total understanding. Yet our society has tended to elevate the head (rational thought) above the heart (emotional response). I want more for my students than a basic education in language arts, mathematics, science, and social studies. I want my students to *feel*, to *dream*, and to *know* they have something to share with the world. This is the process that this art study begins.

REFERENCES

Caine, R. M., & Caine, G. (1994). *Making connections: Teaching and the human brain.* Palo Alto, CA: Addison Wesley.

Down, A. G. (1990). Where are the arts in this adventure called reform? *Virginia Journal of Education, 84*(4), 7–10.

Eisner, E. W. (1981). The role of the arts in cognition and curriculum. *Phi Delta Kappan, 63*(1), 48–52.

Eisner, E. W. (1992, April). The misunderstood role of the arts in human development. *Phi Delta Kappan, 74*(6), 591–595.

Gardner, Howard. (1990). *Art education and human development.* Los Angeles: J. Paul Getty Trust.

Greenfield, E. (1993). *Childtimes: A three generation memoir.* New York: Harper-Collins.

Roser, N. L., & Hoffman, J. V., with L. D. Labbo & C. Farest. (1992). Language charts: A record of story time talk. *Language Arts, 69*(1), 44–52.

CHILDREN'S BOOKS

Agee, Jon. (1988). *The incredible painting of Felix Clousseau.* New York: Farrar, Straus & Giroux.

Biracree, Tom. (1989). *Grandma Moses.* New York: Chelsea House.

Chorao, Kay. (1988). *Cathedral mouse.* New York: Dutton.

dePaola, Tomie. (1991). *Bonjour, Mr. Satie.* New York: Putnam.

Everett, Gwen. (1991). *Li'l sis and Uncle Willie.* New York: Rizzolli.

Hargrove, J. (1990). *Diego Rivera: Mexican Muralist.* Chicago: Childrens Press.

Kesselman, Wendy. (1980). *Emma.* New York: Harper Trophy.

Lawrence, Jacob. (1993). *Harriet and the promised land.* New York: Simon & Schuster. (Original work published 1968)

Lionni, Leo. (1991). *Matthew's dream.* New York: Knopf.

Moore, Clement C. (1991). *The Grandma Moses night before Christmas.* New York: Random House.

Moore, Reavis. (1993). *Native artists of North America.* Santa Fe, NM: John Muir Publications.

Polacco, Patricia. (1991). *Appelemando's dreams.* New York: Philomel.

Ringgold, Faith. (1991). *Tar beach.* New York: Crown.

Ringgold, Faith. (1992). *Aunt Harriet's underground railroad in the sky.* New York: Crown.

Ringgold, Faith. (1993). *Dinner at Aunt Connie's house.* New York: Hyperion.

Sills, Leslie. (1989). *Inspirations: Stories about women artists.* Morton Grove, IL: Albert Whitman.

Strand, Mark. (1986). *Rembrandt takes a walk.* New York: Clarkson N. Potter.

Venezia, Mike. (1990–1992). Getting to Know the World's Greatest Artists series. Series includes: *Salvador Dali, Picasso, van Gogh, Michelangelo, Goya, Botticelli, Rembrandt, Gauguin, Cassatt, Hopper, Monet, Klee, da Vinci.* Chicago: Childrens Press.

A weekend with Diego Rivera. (1994). In A Weekend with the Artists series. New York: Rizzoli International.

Zadrzynska, Ewa. (1990). *The girl with the watering can.* New York: Chameleon.

CHAPTER 4

PicLit

Using Picture Literature to Integrate Language Arts and Content Instruction

Carole Geiger

Today's middle school students have grown up in an action-packed, visual world. They watched a war as it was fought on color televisions in their living rooms. They generally hear and see on their television or computer screen any new information or latest world occurrence. Even their music leaves nothing to imagination, as it is enjoyed with vividly graphic musical videos. It is no wonder that factual, nonpersonal textbook information does little to awaken their interest. Yet a middle school class never fails to respond to the magic of *Catskill Eagle* (Melville, 1991) or to the suspense of Lindbergh's diary of his solo flight across the Atlantic (Burleigh, 1991). A study of flight dynamics and an examination of a time in America's past are naturally integrated by the use of such high-quality picture books.

Many of today's middle school students have not enjoyed the luxury of curling up in someone's lap and savoring a picture book. As the teachers choose appropriate literature for reconnecting curricular concepts, students are also treated to a personal literary experience as they form their own concept of themselves as literate learners. The visual, tactile, and even kinesthetic learner find that picture books, written with high-level text and accuracy, lend understanding to many units of study. As teachers at the middle school level teach with a team concept, picture books that transcend subject boundaries become a natural vehicle for connecting team objectives.

Today's well-written picture books are packed with factual and personal information. They serve in conjunction with the textbook as the personal voice to classroom subject areas. These picture books transcend age, gender, and race. They teach difficult concepts in a personal, honest style. Quality picture books are extensively researched and accurately illustrated, and they complement the classroom curriculum as conversation does a good meal—they are not necessary, but they make it so much more memorable. Literature is able to connect curriculum naturally, modeling vivid writing styles while depicting time, place, people, or scientific facts. Carefully illustrated picture books foster multicultural understanding by carefully accentuating our likenesses as people as well as what makes each of us unique. Thus picture books connect countries, races, and genders as well as providing visual support while discussing international and national issues.

In the following chapter Carole Geiger, a middle school reading specialist, relates ways she shares the magic and versatility of children's literature to spark interest and connect curriculum. She has developed an in-class program, working with each team of teachers for planning purposes and delivering appropriate lessons to entire classes upon request. Collaboration of professionals naturally evolves as she features several picture books a month to correspond with curricular topics being taught. Teachers of all subject areas are included in the weave of literature thread. Fine art classes are enhanced through the use of the art of picture books that demonstrates the medium of study occurring in class, and music classes use picture books that feature the lives and times of famous composers.

Picture books to enhance any subject area can be discovered by involving the classroom community in the search. It is a connection that is contagious. Parents, teachers, and librarians all get caught up in the search. Sharing appropriate printed materials becomes exciting as subject-area facts are taught while students are encouraged to become lifelong seekers of meaning through the printed page. Curriculum is connected for the learner, and personal literacy is fostered.

THE MAGIC OF PICTURE BOOKS

"China!" firmly asserts one student as others sit poised on the edges of their desk chairs, waiting their turns to provide guesses for the brainstorm list growing steadily on the chalkboard. I continue to stroll back and forth across the front of the room, displaying for further concentrated examination the brightly colored cover of today's PicLit selection, David Wisniewski's *Rainplayer* (1991).

"Why?" I encourage, as I write the predicted location.

"Because the buildings look like they're from China," quickly responds the student, carefully scrutinizing the world map mounted with magnets next to the list.

"India!" the next offers with equal certainty, "because the boy's face and clothes look like people from India"—the comment added in response to the encouraging quizzical looks.

"Egypt!" another adds to the list, following the pattern by continuing, "because those markings look like Egyptian writing."

"It has to be a tropical place—just look at those stormy clouds, like maybe a hurricane is coming," explained yet another.

The students' social studies teacher moves quietly around the room, continuing to read silently the free-written paragraphs that hypothesize the location of the story and elaborate the reasons for the hypothesis. She adds a smiley-face to a paper here, encourages a written speculation from an idea-blocked student there, subtly indicating to me when reluctance in a student becomes participation. The whole-class analysis continues, enthusiasm mounting as the list on the board grows longer. Students reinforce one another's observations about geographic features, plant identifications, architecture, clothing, and cultural characteristics. Both of us make a mental note of the wide range of the students' observations. Our objective is to coordinate experiences from which the learner could make connections, an important principle of integrated learning (see Chapter 1), and to keep the lesson progressing smoothly. This could be a geography lesson about boundaries and structures, a science class studying the weather, or a home economics lesson on fabric and fashions; it could be an introduction to foreign-language class, comparing scripts from different times and cultures. However, this lesson is a bridge to the study of ancient Egypt, which activates prior knowledge about native cultures in the Western Hemisphere and refreshes the students' understandings of the criteria they used to study those cultures and on which they will base the study of Egyptian civilization. The students agree to deletions and finally declare the list complete, waiting expectantly as I indicate the correct location of the picture book story on which their thinking and writing lesson centers.

After identification of the location and discussion of the clues in the illustration, the session continues as I once again circulate with the open book, calling the students' attention to the nature of the illustrations while displaying both the cover and selected pages from within. The students' next writing prompt asks them to explain how they think Mr. Wisniewski created the unusual, extraordinarily dramatic artwork for the book. Heads bent, they write. One student peppers his writing with small sketches as part of his explanation. Another remarks that he learned all about the technique in the gifted art program (he was wrong, but he received an "attaboy" for connective thinking).

Answers shared and amazement expressed over the highly detailed, brightly colored cut-and-layered paper illustration in the book, they settle attentively to hear the story read and continue the series of critical thinking prompts that will extend their practice in free-writing clear, concise, focused paragraphs as they draw conclusions, make comparisons and contrasts, predict, analyze, summarize, and hypothesize.

Variations of this activity occur daily in the classes of this particular school. Although this could be an elementary school, or, with adaptation, a high school, in fact these students attend a Virginia middle school. They are sixth-graders, but even seventh- and eighth-graders respond as positively when this same slim volume, *Rainplayer*, is used to stimulate interest in reading, to hone writing skills, and to develop critical thinking skills. It has also been used to pique the interest of teachers in staff development classes and has been shared with adult learners.

Picture books have also worked their magic when used with a learning-disabled eighth-grade boy as we became engrossed together in Jerry Pallotta's *The Furry Alphabet Book* (1986). Intense concentration is shown as we read and discuss, write, and laugh frequently. This time, after three previous failed attempts, this student passes the state literacy test in writing.

These examples demonstrate the magic of picture books with specific, unique features: high-merit literature accompanied by equally high-merit illustrations, selected because the content specifically supports a particular subject-area lesson. Whether the subject be fine arts, performing arts, technology, science, social studies, geography, the environment, mathematics, language arts, or any other of the subject areas taught in our schools, picture literature, what I call PicLit, fills a niche by integrating literature into all content areas. PicLit can provide supplementary information, content elaboration, and avenues for addressing experiential bases, reading needs, writing skills, and thinking expansion across the curriculum.

The brevity of picture books lends itself to content-lesson format. For instance, in one class period, *A River Ran Wild* (Cherry, 1992) could supplement a lesson about Native American history, factories and how they affect the environment, or the settling of the northeastern United States. PicLit provides pertinent information succinctly and compellingly. A teacher can choose to use a particular book for part of an instructional time period or more than one period. This literary category is highly flexible and easy to adapt to various instructional needs and purposes.

Another positive characteristic is that the presentation of PicLit enhances both the retention and incorporation of information by students. Few can resist the lure of David Wisniewski's *Sundiata* (1992) as it reveals the twists and turns of an important era in African history in succinctly expressive prose, combined with the impact of his unique shadow-play illustrations. How easy it becomes to remember the environmental lessons entwined in Lynne Cherry's *The Great Kapok Tree* (1990), with her excellent sense of story enhanced by a density of accurately detailed artwork as she weaves a valid, instructional tale. Students in music class, drama, or Russian studies surely remember more effectively when exposed to Rachel Isadora's adaptation of *Swan Lake* (1991), with its exquisite impressionistic paintings. Math block might become a scourge of the past if more students were exposed regularly to the delights of mathematics-related PicLit, such as Ted Rand's (1993) version of Carl Sandburg's *Arithmetic*.

Picture books meet the interests and needs of any age group. Graeme Base may have had young children in mind when creating *Animalia* (1986), but all ages find his details utterly fascinating. Many of the folk tales, myths, and legends of diverse cultures can be found in scholarly tomes intended for serious study, but most adults share children's delight in exploring less intimidating, more visually appealing versions of those same literary pieces. Age or grade designations on a book or in a review must be seen as guides for independent reading only, because these ageless books appeal to all readers. *The Crane Wife* (Yagawa, 1979), *The Girl Who Loved Caterpillars* (Merrill, 1992), *The Legend of the Bluebonnet* (dePaola, 1983), *The Legend of the Indian Paintbrush* (dePaola, 1988), and *The Winged Cat: A Tale of Ancient Egypt* (Lattimore, 1992) are just a few examples of time-tested favorites for all ages.

SELECTING PICLIT

The first step in beginning to use picture books with older children is to make careful book choices. The following are criteria to keep in mind as a teacher considers the literary and artistic standards of books for PicLit selections:

- **Select exquisitely illustrated books that meet a high standard for literary and artistic merit.** For example, Boccaccio undoubtedly smiles broadly across the eons in William Wise's adaptation of *The Black Falcon* (1990), perfect to include in studies of the Middle Ages. Bill Martin and John Arbuthnot have entwined life lessons and culture memorably in *Knots on a Counting Rope* (1987), appropriate for studies of family, Native Americans, or the handicapped.
- **Select books that make content relevant in a manner obvious enough not to confuse students.** An unabridged collection of Shakespeare's works might discourage most students, but *The Bard of Avon: The Story of William Shakespeare* (Stanley, 1992) breaks the ice and makes further study of Shakespeare exciting. *The Bard of Avon* is a good example

of selecting a book with multiple instructional possibilities or subjects, such as medieval society, building and construction, or theater styles and history.

- **Select books that will activate prior knowledge and connect it with new lessons to compensate for missing experiential background.** For instance, alphabet books can provide a transition from the known to the new in any subject area. *The Z Was Zapped* (Van Allsburg, 1987) fits into a drama lesson, possibly lessening students' self-consciousness as they ease themselves into dramatic presentation. Jane Yolen's *Elfabet* (1990a) could introduce a language arts lesson on fantasy or spark student creativity in illustrating fantasy for an art assignment. James Rice's *Texas Alphabet* (1988) could ease the way for distinguishing between fact and fiction in studying the West. Cathi Hepworth's *ANTics* (1992) might pique interest in a zoology unit on insects. Alphabet books aren't the only type to fill this need, though. *Follow the Dream: The Story of Christopher Columbus* (Sis, 1991) can remind students of earlier studies before delving more deeply into exploration, colonization, or the history of the Western Hemisphere. *Kiana's Iditarod* (Gill, 1984) might precede a mature study of Alaska and such cultural specifics as dog sledding. *Seven Blind Mice* (Young, 1992) could ease the transition to an affective unit or encourage sensitivity to colors in art.
- **Carefully establish for yourself the purpose for the content of the PicLit chosen so that you will be able to guide the students to see how the book fits into the study.** If students see only entertainment value in a book, they tend to shuffle information straight through their short-term memories. Consider the exciting retelling of *Ali Baba and the Forty Thieves* (McVitty, 1988), and *Wings* (Yolen, 1991). *Ali Baba* enhances a unit on Middle Eastern studies and provides balance for those whose only previous experience with that area of the world involves a movie character named Aladdin. Dennis Nolan's extraordinary illustrations in *Wings* cement the characters firmly into the viewers' memories and make the ancient Greek world come alive.
- **Evaluate the physical size and visual clarity of the books.** The edition should be large enough to be seen and appreciated at a distance around the classroom as it is presented. The size of the book itself and the clarity of the illustrations should catch student attention from the front of the classroom and as the reader walks around the instructional setting reading the displayed book. Charles Santore's large-format, magnificently illustrated version of *Aesop's Fables* (1988) is very easy to see. However, Jerry Pallotta's small alphabet books fit a special niche in developing vocabulary and concepts [for instance, *The Underwater Alphabet Book* (1991b) in science or *The Icky Bug Counting Book* (1986) in

mathematics]. Their generally clear, distinct illustrations compensate for the size limitations of the books themselves and merit adapted use with a large group.

- **Avoid books that appear to mimic television cartoons or comic book format.** Students routinely overdose themselves on intellectually confining and visually limiting media. Even quality cartoon-style illustrations may be too indistinct to be appreciated by large groups. As a positive model, *Johnny Appleseed* (Kellogg, 1988) qualifies on its literary and artistic merits and contributes well to American studies.

- **Be flexible in the assignment of age and grade classifications for books.** Almost any book can be used with almost any age group if the adaptation of the presentation meets the learning needs of your target group. One of the outstanding features of PicLit is that it transcends generational boundaries. Ignore the traditional or commonly agreed-upon age and grade assignments whenever it suits instructional purposes. *The Quilt Story* (Johnston, 1985), *Nettie's Trip South* (Turner, 1987), and *Ragtime Tumpie* (Schroeder, 1989) adapt equally well to a classroom of primary learners, high school social studies or fine arts classes, or adult learning settings. The teacher's preparation, presentation, attitude, and clarity of purpose make all the difference in student acceptance of the works read to them.

- **Use reasoned judgment and always preview.** Not only should professional judgment prevail regarding such important factors as content applicability, quality of art and literature, length, and size of the book, but specific community characteristics and the policies of the school or administrative division should apply. Occasionally the content of a particular book might not be appropriate for a particular group of learners or for the community served by a class or school. Teacher caution and expertise should forever be professional partners.

- **Develop a sixth sense for sources of picture literature.** School librarians and media specialists routinely keep informed about new releases, collect "wish lists" from faculty and staff for future orders, and derive ardent personal and professional satisfaction from sharing what they know about the types of books available that meet specific curricular needs. Fine arts teachers, technology faculty, and specialists frequently note unique and age-appropriate books available in their area of expertise. Publications from professional sources, such as the International Reading Association, the American Library Association, and the National Council of Teachers of English, regularly provide invaluable lists. Make regular rounds of book stores, establishing rapport with the staff, who become willing collaborators in the quest for just the right books, even when they're on the discount tables. Haunt yard sales, library support group sales, and thrift shops in search of literary treasures. It becomes a comfortable, fulfilling habit always to have an eye cocked for a potential source of superb picture literature.

PREPARING STUDENTS FOR PICLIT: THE BASICS

At the beginning of this chapter, I described a class of sixth-graders being introduced to a picture book in order to extend their writing and thinking skills using content-relevant information. The vignette presented followed a carefully planned series of activities and questions designed to elicit the desired outcomes. The following basic guidelines provide a loose framework that can be manipulated to meet individual requirements.

- **Provide an introductory activity.** Possibilities include placing the story in time, guiding students to determine the relationship to current time, and/or placing the story on a world map. Students might do this on a class wall map, on a cooperative group map, or on individual, acetate-covered desk maps that they can write on and reuse. Encourage the student to speculate about the title, predicting what the book is about, how it will relate to the subject matter, or what special meaning it might involve. Such speculation should vary in format: written answers to a teacher question one time, a group written response another time, or whole-class brainstorming with answers on the board yet another time. Consider creating a KWL (what I Know, what I Want to learn, what I have Learned) chart and completing the K column in order to activate prior knowledge (Ogle, 1986). Brainstorm lists, free-writes, and webs provide that activation, too.
- **Guide students to relate the theme, setting, plot, characters, time, or other characteristics of the story to various content areas, emphasizing your particular content purposes.** Group discussion, individual or group writing, and individual written responses to a dictated question fulfill this purpose. As necessary, further guide students to relate the story to what they already know in order to retrieve stored knowledge and provide a foundation for building new understandings. Again, using such techniques as creating webs, completing graphic organizers, or retelling a previously mastered process, event, or story satisfies this requirement.
- **Incorporate various modes of expression through writing.** This might include drawing or sketching; labeling; mapping, webbing, and clustering; listing; doodling; writing sentence responses or paragraph responses; expanding sentences or paragraphs; completing framed para-

graphs; and creating KWLs. Remember that some children seem to learn and retain information more effectively when allowed to draw, doodle, or otherwise express themselves on paper while listening at the same time.

- **Create writing opportunities that require development of higher-level thinking skills.** These skills include comparisons and contrasts, prediction, analysis, and drawing conclusions, among others. Judicious use of analogies provides more bridges from prior knowledge to the new.
- **Vary the writing challenges.** The possibilities include creating new endings, summarizing, "reading between the lines," presenting character sketches, explaining, dissenting—whatever your mind or the students' can devise. View PicLit as a venue for giving them permission to let their minds soar.

To illustrate the basic guidelines presented to prepare students, I offer two examples of lessons that I have used in middle school classrooms to introduce carefully selected picture books.

North Country Night: An Example

North Country Night, written and illustrated by Daniel San Souci (1990), makes an excellent vehicle for studying wildlife and weather in science while practicing writing skills in elaboration, selecting relevant information, providing details, and establishing tone. The following lesson, used with appropriate adaptations in the sixth, seventh, and eighth grades, zeros in on animal studies while providing an opportunity to apply writing skills in response to a specific prompt.

This lesson incorporates science, reading, writing, and the use of reference materials. It would, therefore, take several different class periods to implement and complete. At the discretion of the teacher, completing the assignment could be homework or it could be entirely done in class.

The students' first exposure to the book reveals the unusual nature of the illustrations. Using a discussion format, the group explores the reasons for the use of the blue background throughout to illustrate night and the differences in how things look at night versus in daylight.

All the animals presented in the book are listed on a chart, along with terms such as *nocturnal* that will be useful in discussing the animals and the book. This chart is mounted on the back of a world map. For use later, but initially not in sight, is a map of the United States.

After briefly introducing the vocabulary, the teacher reads the book, pausing to encourage comments, to point out details in the pictures, and to ask general questions about the animals. It is important to circulate throughout the room while reading and displaying the illustrations so all students have an opportunity to be involved with the book itself and to appreciate the beauty of the illustrations.

The students attempt their first writing–thinking activity: They speculate about where the story takes place, using what they know about terrain, the animals in the story, and any clues provided in the book. They complete this assignment as a free-write, with opportunity to ask questions but without the need to do research. Collaboration might be desirable, but each student should produce an individual written response.

The world map serves initially for students to identify the area of the world where the story takes place, with the teacher providing background information as needed, depending on the age of the students. Once the students have determined that the story takes place in the United States, the teacher can display the U.S. map and further guide them to eliminate their suggested places until they narrow the field to the northwest United States (most probably northern California).

Involved, the students now receive the writing prompt: "Select one of the animals in the story. Write a description of that animal's nighttime activities and adventures." Reference books, textbooks, and other zoology teaching materials may be made available for the students to use. If desired, each student prepares a KWL chart at this time.

Now students begin the writing process, with teacher guidance and instruction. Time well spent involves the teacher guiding creation of a web as the pre-write. Each student completes a web with individually selected information and details, using reference books as needed.

All students write several examples of expanded descriptions and post them for the others to critique and use as models. This provides additional opportunities to expand student use of adverbs and adjectives and to convert ordinary words into vivid vocabulary. They might write them on the chalkboard, post them on a bulletin board or section of classroom wall, or present them in cooperative groups. Or they might dictate them to a group leader or to the teacher to be written on the overhead projector or the chalkboard. Fellow students then suggest changes or compliment effective phrasing.

Now they are ready to write the rough drafts, using the webs for their organization and the expanded descriptions as a basis for elaboration of the prompt. Following the steps of the writing process, peer or teacher conferencing leads to editing, as many times as necessary before the final step begins. Oral reading of the rough draft to a peer editor or taking turns reading one another's drafts aloud works particularly well to speed up the editing process. At last, that final step arrives. Each student writes a final copy, proofreads it, and "publishes" the work by sharing it. If a younger class is available, students enjoy reading their stories to those children. Some teachers encourage their writers to read their own works aloud to a group or to the whole class. Others allow peer readers to make the presentation. Another variation incorporates volunteers (parents, other faculty, or administrators), who visit to read aloud or silently or to listen to readings of the completed student writings.

Sky Dogs: An Example

Jane Yolen's *Sky Dogs* (1990b) complements a unit of Native American studies or environmental issues. The following questioning strategy sparks student interest in a culture and forms of expression very different from today's.

Again using maps, the teacher orients the students to the Great Plains area of the United States before the story begins. As usual, the teacher briefly presents key vocabulary. It is important not to show students the cover of the book or any of the interior illustrations before beginning to read.

As the Sky Dogs enter the story, the students respond in writing to the question, "Who or what do you think Sky Dogs are? Explain why you think as you do." After a few minutes of free-writing, they share responses orally (without teacher affirmation or denial) and then the teacher continues to read the story.

The story continues with more references to Sky Dogs and the teacher states, "Add to or change your explanation of Sky Dogs." The oral sharing of free-writing responses occurs one or two more times before the teacher confirms the correct answer by showing the students the book cover and accompanying illustrations. By this time, a large proportion of the students will have figured out that Sky Dogs are horses—and they'll be downright proud of themselves in the process.

Students come up with some very innovative ideas, such as the following examples, which represent the variety of responses that have occurred during different presentations of this book:

> Sky Dogs might mean that is what they worship.
> Sky Dogs might mean that the sky dogs came out of the tall sky-scraping mountains in the middle of the sky.
> Sky Dogs might mean what it would be like if the Indians died and went into the sky but keep on roaming and running just like dogs.

A similar approach helps students develop the concept entailed in the term *Old Man's sleeping room,* used a number of times in the story. Students come up with some interesting responses for this one, too:

Old Man's sleeping room means a dark place where no one has
been in a long time. It's a quiet place like an old man.
Old Man's sleeping room means the old man who loves horses
and the old man is dead.
Old Man's sleeping room probably means that it's a retirement
home for old men or a church for old people.

Understanding and relating to terms like *Sky Dogs* and *Old Man's sleeping room* must precede any meaningful involvement with the text and the
connections the teacher wishes to make to content objectives. Getting students involved in determining meaning increases their ability to make
meaningful associations and enhances the likelihood that they will remember the pertinent concept.

PICLIT AND CONTENT: A SYNERGISTIC RELATIONSHIP

Quality picture books can provide numerous opportunities for students to
relate current content-area literature to previously studied content-area
literature and other types of reading materials. When picture books are
used with enthusiasm, students' learning is enhanced and their appreciation of both the literature and the content develops. Philosophers, poets,
theologians, and atheists alike have extolled the intrinsic value of the
beautiful in sound, word, and picture through the ages. Authors and illustrators today revalidate that importance as they create literary works of
art for readers of all ages in picture book format. On the shelves of bookstores and libraries everywhere, the book-browsing public can indulge their
intellects and spirits in the elegant and artistic pages of volumes addressing content-area categories as varied as the subjects we teach. Picture books
offer an invigorating and illuminating new dimension in teaching content
area, whatever subject it might be. When a PicLit book is discovered to fit
a lesson, it is enjoyable and challenging to devise a plan for using that book,
and learning will become more enjoyable and memorable for everyone
involved.

REFERENCE

Ogle, D. (1986). KWL: A teaching model that develops active reading of expository text. *The Reading Teacher, 39,* 564–470.

PICLIT

Base, Graeme. (1986). *Animalia*. New York: Abrams.

Burleigh, R. (1991). *Flight*. Illustrated by Mike Wimmer. New York: Philomel.

Cherry, Lynne. (1990). *The great kapok tree*. San Diego: Harcourt Brace Javonovich.

Cherry, Lynne. (1992). *A river ran wild*. San Diego: Harcourt Brace Jovanovich.

dePaola, Tomie. (1983). *The legend of the bluebonnet*. New York: Putnam.

dePaola, Tomie. (1988). *The legend of the Indian paintbrush*. New York: Putnam.

Gill, Shelley. (1984). *Kiana's iditarod*. Homer, AK: Paws IV Publishing.

Hepworth, Cathi. (1992). *ANTics*. New York: Putnam.

Isadora, Rachel. (1991). *Swan lake*. New York: Putnam.

Johnston, Tony. (1985). *The quilt story*. Illustrated by Tomie dePaola. New York: Putnam.

Kellogg, Steven. (1988). *Johnny Appleseed*. New York: Morrow.

Lattimore, Deborah Nourse. (1992). *The winged cat: A tale of ancient Egypt*. New York: HarperCollins.

Martin, Bill, & Arbuthnot, John.(1987). *Knots on a counting rope*. Illustrated by Ted Rand. New York: Holt.

McVitty, Walter. (1988). *Ali Baba and the forty thieves*. Illustrated by Margaret Early. New York: Abrams.

Melville, H. (1991). *Catskill eagle*. Paintings by Thomas Locker. New York: Philomel.

Merrill, Jean. (1992). *The girl who loved caterpillars*. New York: Philomel.

Pallotta, Jerry. (1986). *The icky bug counting book*. Watertown, MA: Charlesbridge.

Pallotta, Jerry. (1991a). *The furry alphabet book*. Watertown, MA: Charlesbridge.

Pallotta, Jerry. (1991b). *The underwater alphabet book*. Watertown, MA: Charlesbridge.

Rand, Ted. (1993). *Carl Sandburg: Arithmetic*. San Diego: Harcourt Brace Jovanovich.

Rice, James. (1988). *Texas alphabet*. Gretna, LA: Pelican.

San Souci, Daniel. (1990). *North country night*. New York: Doubleday.

Santore, Charles. (1988). *Aesop's fables*. New York: Crown.

Schroeder, Alan. (1989). *Ragtime Tumpie*. Boston: Little, Brown.

Sis, Peter. (1991). *Follow the dream: The story of Chrisopher Columbus*. New York: Knopf.

Stanley, Diane. (1992). *The bard of Avon: The story of William Shakespeare*. Illustrated by Peter Venema. New York: Morrow.

Turner, Ann. (1987). *Nettie's trip south*. Illustrated by Ronald Himler. New York: Macmillan.

Van Allsburg, Chris. (1987). *The Z was zapped*. Boston: Houghton Mifflin.

Wise, William. (1990). *The black falcon*. Illustrated by Gillian Barlow. New York: Philomel.

Wisniewski, David. (1991). *Rainplayer*. Boston: Houghton Mifflin.

Wisniewski, David. (1992). *Sundiata*. Boston: Houghton Mifflin.

Yagawa, Sumiko. (1979). *The crane wife*. Translated by K. Paterson. Illustrated by S. Akaba. New York: Morrow.

Yolen, Jane. (1990a). *Elfabet: An ABC of elves*. Illustrated by Lauren Mills. Boston: Little, Brown.

Yolen, Jane. (1990b). *Sky Dogs*. Illustrated by Barry Moser. San Diego: Harcourt Brace Jovanovich.

Yolen, Jane. (1991). *Wings*. Illustrated by Dennis Nolan. San Diego: Harcourt Brace Jovanovich.

Young, Ed. (1992). *Seven blind mice*. New York: Philomel.

CHAPTER 5

A Schoolwide Study
of Stars and Skies

Bette Bosma

The all-school study described in this chapter demonstrates how research projects can be effectively adapted and used in the classroom by creative and competent teachers. The stars and skies material that formed the basis for the schoolwide three-week study was developed as an ESEA title IV project (Bosworth et al., 1979) and was written for grades 4–8. The Rehoboth teachers revised and adapted the study to fit kindergarten through grade 6.

Located on the edge of the Navajo reservation in New Mexico, Rehoboth Christian School was formerly a mission school but is now parent-owned by Christian Native Americans, Anglos, and Hispanics. The elementary school population is 65% Navajo, 10% Hispanic, and 25% Anglo. Integration of curriculum was a natural step for the Rehoboth teachers because they adopted a literature-based reading program in 1985 that gradually included writing, language patterning, and spelling. Finding books to match themes and subject areas was a common practice, but planning a thematic unit with schoolwide integration required a high level of connectedness. Through teachers' communicating, coordinating, and collaborating, students gained a unified view of learning and its purpose.

My association with this school began in 1984, when I brought a group of Calvin College students there to study a multicultural approach to the teaching of reading. I returned three times with groups of students and twice as a volunteer consultant to help the teachers make the transition to an integrated approach to curriculum. When I returned in 1993, I found them immersed in the study of the solar system, and my involvement was limited to observation and encouragement. I was very impressed with the caliber of writing that the students at all grade levels produced during the study.

The collaboration of the teachers was particularly helpful for the new faculty members. The cooperation of the city of Gallup library and the local public school district enhanced the collaborative nature of the project. The Gallup–McKinley County school district loaned Rehoboth School StarLab,* an inflatable planetarium and supporting resources. One of the Rehoboth teachers received training with StarLab and in turn trained the other teachers. He coordinated the use of the lab with the Gallup–McKinley schools.

This was the second year that Rehoboth planned an all-school study of stars and skies. The coordinators reported that it fell into place more easily this time. The entire staff met to discuss and share ideas for the unit, under the direction of the teacher who had received the StarLab training. Native American legends were an important part of the study. Cultivating the imagination was as important an objective for each classroom as the acquisition of information.

The focal point of the schoolwide study was the portable StarLab. The 16-foot diameter plastic dome was set up in an all-purpose area in the center of the school. The planetarium inflation fan at the end of one tunnel kept the structure in place, and the classes entered through another tunnel. The ecliptic projector was placed on a storage stand which held the numerous star and constellation cylinders. Pointer flashlight and regular flashlight usage made the stellar objects easy to spot.

Since the children walked past the planetarium every day, they could hardly wait for their turn to visit. The teachers chose to schedule several short visits into the lab rather than long periods of instruction, based on their experience from the previous year. Each visit stimulated many questions that could be answered by subsequent visits or in the many books the teachers had collected. The favorite book of all the teachers and classes was *They Dance in the Sky: Native American Star Myths* by Jean G. Monroe and Ray A. Williamson (1987). The one copy, loaned by a high school teacher, was in constant demand, and all ages loved hearing the stories. High on the list of changes for the next year is to have multiple copies of this popular book.

Since this was the second year with the StarLab, plans were carefully coordinated so that the learning in each classroom would build on the investigations of the prior year. The general objectives of the study were reinforced through the grades, elaborated upon and extended to fit the developmental levels of the students. The teachers built in enough flexibility so that they could explore the particular interests of the students.

---

*Copyright for the StarLab Planetarium System is held by Learning Technologies, Inc., 59 Walden Street, Cambridge, Massachusetts.

In this chapter, I describe the approach taken in each grade to show how varied, but also how connected, the study was. References to many book titles are included so that readers can benefit from the extensive search the Rehoboth teachers made to provide authentic and stimulating reading material.

KINDERGARTEN: STAR GAZERS

The kindergartners became avid star gazers. The first trip to the StarLab lasted only a few minutes to get the children used to sitting in the dark and learning where the star lights would be appearing. This made them comfortable and eager for repeat visits. When they learned that the second-graders who were their reading partners were also visiting the lab, they experienced a strong sense of truly belonging to the school. Since their classroom was in a separate building, the walk to the main building added to their excitement.

The main emphasis of the kindergarten's study was stars: star size, birth of stars, major constellations, and major stars. Native American names were used whenever possible along with the Greek names if those were known, such as North Fire (North Star), Revolving Male (Big Dipper), Revolving Female (Cassiopeia), and Dilyehe (Pleiades).

The kindergartners acted out the birth of a star with creative movement. They illustrated Psalm 148: "Praise the Lord . . . sun and moon, praise him, all you shining stars." Language expression advanced through their careful descriptions of the position of stars and constellations that they saw in the StarLab and through their oral storytelling. Math concepts of size and distance became easier to understand through repeated exposure to Schwartz's *How Much Is a Million?* (1985).

In addition to reading and retelling the myths from *They Dance in the Sky* (Monroe & Williamson, 1987), the kindergarten teacher read to the class *The Sky Is Full of Stars* (Branley, 1981), *Mystery of the Navajo Moon* (Green, 1991), and *Follow the Drinking Gourd* (Winter, 1988). References that the children browsed through and shared with their parents included Ranger Rick's *Mission to Planet Earth* (1992), Dinah Moche's *What's Up There* (1975), *Stars* (1988), and Thompson's *Glow in the Dark Constellations* (1989). The teacher wrote about her favorite parts of the study:

One day we went into the StarLab and looked at the Native American constellations. The children took turns pointing out constellations as I told the legends. I didn't have a legend for each constellation, so I asked them to make their own legend. One little boy who is very quiet in the classroom told two beautiful legends. Back in the classroom, we used star stickers to make our own constellations. Then as a group we composed a legend describing how this constellation ended up in the sky. I invited the parents and students to view the StarLab together one evening. The kindergarten children were able to show their parents the location of the major stars and constellations. The literature, reference books, and charts we made were available for parents and children to look through together. The whole evening was a real learning experience and a confidence builder.

GRADE 1: SPACE TRAVELERS

The first-graders zeroed in on each major body of the stars and skies and learned the place of the earth in the solar system. The study of constellations and myths was extended to include more star formations and Greek myths as well as Native American legends. Bible study centered on God as creator and all of creation praising Him.

Art and math learning were integrated in the building of space ships that took them into space each day. The first-grade teacher sent a letter home asking parents to help their children find containers or large pieces of cardboard that could be made into imaginary spaceships. Every child brought a box or cylinder that was ingeniously transformed with glue, colored paper, paint, fabric, and a variety of found objects into an individual spaceship. Building the ships used all the adding, subtracting, and measuring skill the first-graders possessed. Some of the ships were big enough to sit in, but many were models that the children pretended to ride. The ships were parked on every available surface in the room. Their imaginary trips were planned carefully. Based on information they learned about the planet they were to visit, they decided what to wear and what essentials they would take with them.

Language arts/reading time found the children listening to myths and poetry, writing stories about the pretend trip into space, and reading individual space books. The poetry included found poems as well as those created by the children. Social studies developed into learning about astronauts, especially Neil Armstrong and his life.

The first-grade teacher checked out a variety of space information books from the public library, which the children used intensely. She read aloud the D'Aulaires' *Book of Greek Myths* (1962), Udry's *The Moon Jumpers* (1959), Green's *Mystery of the Navajo Moon* (1991), Winter's *Follow the Drink-*

ing Gourd (1988), and Yolen's Commander Toad Adventure books (1980–1987). The first-grade teacher wrote:

> Making our space ships and traveling first to the sun, then to the other bodies in the solar system really got them thinking about how each would feel (hot, cold, etc.). They also really retained a lot of information about each and could compare and contrast each place we visited. The imagination is a fun thing to work with.

GRADE 2: TREKKIES

The sun, planets, stars, and constellations comprised the heart of the second-grade study. The enterprising teacher formed a natural tie-in with his preceding African American history unit by reading Winter's *Follow the Drinking Gourd* (1988) and Monjo's *The Drinking Gourd* (1970/1983) and guiding the discussion to the stars that provided direction for the escaping slaves.

In planning the integrated unit in grade 2, the teacher emphasized previously taught strategies that the children could now practice and new strategies that he would teach to refine their skills and concept learning.

The second-graders used the KWL strategy (Ogle, 1986) with planet information books. Before reading, the whole class brainstormed what they knew (K), the first step of the strategy. The K information was recorded on the first column of a chart, evidence of the children's prior knowledge. They generated questions for what they wanted to know (W) and to clarify some of the information in the first column that was confusing. The W questions, placed in the second column, set the purpose for the children's individual reading and exploration. During reading the second-graders found the answers to their questions and reaffirmed or altered their information in the K(now) column. After reading, the readers contributed their findings and filled out the third column with what they had learned (L). The KWL strategy had been taught to the children before this study, and they were now able to practice this new thinking skill.

Using their knowledge of how authors develop characters, the second-graders compared the realistic characters in books such as *The Drinking Gourd* (Winter, 1988) with the fantasy characters in the Commander Toad series (Yolen, 1980–87) and the spirit characters in the traditional myths and legends. Legends read to the class included *Star Boy* and *Her Seven Brothers* by Goble (1983, 1988) and *They Dance in the Sky* by Monroe and Williamson (1987). They made character webs of Commander Toad and his crew members. The character study gave the children the confidence to invent their own characters for their creative stories. They used story mapping to organize their ideas. They placed their invented characters within a setting of time and place, planned a problem the characters would face, and jotted down episodes that would happen on the way to the resolution of the problem.

Math time found the second-graders estimating distances in space. Thinking in big numbers helped them see the need for learning place values. They really stretched their knowledge of place value by figuring out the gigantic numbers used in astronomy. *How Much Is a Million?* (Schwartz, 1985) was helpful in offering a visual way to imagine the vastness of space and the number of stars.

The second-grade teacher used "Oobleck," described in *Great Explorations in Math and Science* (Berman & Fairwell, 1988). He recounted:

> I used this ["Oobleck"] along with the Dr. Seuss book about
> Oobleck to introduce students to the idea of exploring other
> planets. Students studied Oobleck, made with corn starch, water,
> and food coloring, agreed on how it acts, and then designed a
> spaceship to land there. We also made creatures adapted to the
> planet Oobleck.
>
> Commander Toad was a favorite. Students loved to repeat,
> "Commander Toad, Brave and Bright, Bright and Brave." I knew it
> would be a hit since I had five trekkies in my classroom.

After the total class activities described above, the teacher divided the class into eight teams. Their task was to find and share information about one planet. The teams discussed what to look for before they began reading. Then they dug into learning on their own, using books on tapes, easy readers, read alouds, and illustrated information books on planets. Each team filled a big chart with data on their planet: name, color, temperatures, surface type, and other categories they had chosen. All this new knowledge led some children to make changes in their Oobleck creatures to make them able to visit the planet their team had studied. Others edited their stories to make the imaginary planets fit their new scientific knowledge (a mark of good fantasy writing!). Exciting new inventions included vehicles for traveling around the planet.

The children's enthusiasm for writing led them to compose a whole-class story about Commander Toad coming to the planet Oobleck and individual stories about Commander Toad visiting their special planet. Children continued to read and reread stories about space, and the teacher made a gradual transition into the next unit of study.

GRADES 3 AND 4: PLANET BUILDERS

The third- and fourth-grade teachers planned their units together, and projects ranged from individual story writing to interclass art displays. The culminating activity was arranging their papier-mâché, accurately scaled planets outdoors in proper space and sequence. Fortunately, there was a large field behind the school.

The fourth-level science objectives, offered in the curriculum project guide (Bosworth et al., 1979, p. 3), were used by both classes. In the StarLab, the classes began by identifying the cardinal directions within the planetarium and the location of the North Star. The students were able to describe the general east-to-west movement of the sun, stars, and moon, and observe and describe the apparent motion of the Big Dipper in relation to the North Star. They learned to observe and discuss the concept that stars continually shine but may not be seen by the naked eye due to other, stronger light sources. Constellation study centered on the movement of constellations and demonstrations that the constellations are imaginary star groupings that are not connected in any physical way. A constellation-connected projection drum within the portable planetarium made it possible to identify the circumpolar constellations.

Learning for both classes extended far beyond those objectives. Language arts/reading objectives focused on locating written and visual information, researching, summarizing findings, report writing, reading legends and myths for pleasure, and writing their own stories. Studying the landform of the planets fit fourth-grade objectives for social studies. Both classes reinforced and extended their concept of spatial relationships as well as their ability to chart and graph by drawing comparisons of sizes and distances. The fourth-graders applied their new knowledge of decimals in their report writing. Bible study related God's role and majesty to facts about the universe.

The D'Aulaires' *Book of Greek Myths* (1962) provided stories to contrast and compare with their familiar Native American legends. Informational books included *Seeing Earth from Space* (Lauber, 1990) and *Voyager to the Planets* (Apfel, 1991).

The third-grade teacher recounted that his most successful part of the study was

[the children's] orientation to the night sky. Students became very good at recognizing and locating constellations. We worked hard at having them be able to verbally describe a constellation's position using directionality and relationships to other stars. This is not an easy thing to do, even for adults.

The fourth-grade teacher felt that the best part was that

> when doing the planets the children thought of them as their own planet. Two groups did each planet and during class discussion when they presented their planets, information would sometimes differ. They would go back on their own and double check. Making them responsible for teaching their planet to the others worked well.

GRADE 5: ASTRONOMERS

Having been introduced to the major constellations the previous year, the fifth-graders were ready to learn about an array of star formations. Partners selected a constellation after an initial introduction in the StarLab and decided on three questions that they wanted to answer. Limiting their research yielded succinct, factual information that they shared with their classmates and made looking in tables of contents and indexes less overwhelming. Topic and detail sentence concepts were reviewed before the reports were begun, and the students met a challenge to write clear, interesting paragraphs. The book that was most in demand for question answering was Jacqueline and Simon Mitton's *Concise Book of Astronomy* (1978). Their explanation of basic astronomy concepts fit fifth-graders very well. Other popular titles were Moche's *What's Up There: Questions and Answers About Stars and Space* (1975); *Big Book of Stars and Planets* by Robin Kerrod (1988); Branley's *The Sky Is Full of Stars* (1981); and Reigot's *A Book About Planets and Stars* (1988), which contained five chapters loaded with information: "The Solar System," "The Inner Planets," "The Outer Planets," "The Stars," and a chapter on technology entitled "What Next." Fifth-grade knowledge of science and math was stretched when the researchers absorbed star facts such as distance in light-years, magnitude, and the place of the individual stars in the constellation.

The teacher read aloud daily, choosing Native American legends from Monroe and Williamson's *They Dance in the Sky* (1987), and myths from the D'Aulaires' *Book of Greek Myths* (1962). Special favorites from the Greek myths were the stories of Cepheus and Cassiopeia and about Orion the Hunter. The stories were fascinating, and the constellations were easy to find. Soon all the students were writing their own legends and myths and drawing real or imaginary constellations.

The highlight of the study for the teacher and the class was the StarLab itself. A student wrote, "I thought it was wonderful! Going into the star lab was so neat. I learned a lot more than I thought I would."

The teacher agreed and added:

The entire study provided real-world learning. Best of all, it allowed parents and children a terrific opportunity to spend time together finding stars and constellations. On the Friday before the unit began, the students constructed star-finders using the Sky Calendar from Abrams Planetarium, Michigan State University, East Lansing, MI. Constructing these out of tagboard and a photocopy of the night sky was great fun. I assigned the students to choose an evening over the weekend in which to take a parent out to a dark area and use the star/constellation finder. The students came to school Monday bubbling with stories of stars they had found and what fun they'd had with a dad or mom or even grandma! This one activity set the stage for the entire study. Their interest had been piqued. Several parents reported an insistence on the part of their children to go out each evening the next week. Many parents related that their children taught them much they hadn't known. It was gratifying for me to see so many of the parents working with their children on a unified, educational venture that was beneficial to both parent and child.

One fifth-grader wrote a note to his teacher:

I really enjoyed this study a lot and I wish it could last longer. My favorite part about it was learning about some of the constellations and going home and finding them. I loved going into StarLab and being able to see and understand the stars better. I also liked to do the research and everything else we did this week. Thank you for letting my mom come to school. She really enjoyed it.

CONSTELLATIONS IN GRADE 6

The social studies/language arts teacher and the math/science teacher collaborated to present an interdisciplinary study for the sixth-graders. Books were borrowed from the public library to read for both pleasure and information, and to provide new sources to satisfy the curiosity stimulated by the trips to the StarLab. These were shared by other grades as well. A complete list of the books appears at the end of this chapter.

The math/science teacher emphasized measuring the distance of stars from earth, latitude, star positions, and angles. The language arts teacher monitored small groups reporting to each other on myths and legends and comparing the explanations for the constellations made by various Native American tribes, Greeks, and Romans. Both imaginative and factual writing was an important part of their study. The class worked on correct spelling of numerous astronomy-related words. The language arts teacher explained:

> The researching/writing reports and doing projects was most successful because of the wide range of topics selected by students. The activity was easily adapted to the wide range of abilities. Students selected topics and used books from elementary, high school, and Gallup libraries to do their research. They worked in small groups with others interested in the same topic. Next year I will have the students visit the Gallup library and choose their own books for research before the StarLab arrives.

A favorite set of books for independent reading was Isaac Asimov's Library of the Universe series (1988–1991). They were also reading novels such as *Sing Down the Moon* (O'Dell, 1970), legends and myths, and biographies such as *Sally Ride* (Behrens, 1984) and *Women in Space* (Briggs, 1988). The teacher read aloud a Cochiti myth, "Coyote Scatters the Stars"; a Snohomish myth, "The Elk Hunters"; and a Kiowa myth, "The Fixed Star"—all from the StarLab manual (Bosworth et al., 1979). The sixth-graders wrote myths about a constellation they chose when they were in the StarLab. Later they went back into StarLab and told their original myths in the dark, pointing at their constellation with the penlight.

CONCLUSION

Engaging the entire school in a topical study provided a sense of community that was demonstrated both by family involvement and by a camaraderie among the younger and older students. Everyone was interested in the third- and fourth-graders' outdoor display of model planets. Children from various classes compared their visits to StarLab. References to what they had learned last year showed that students were using previous knowledge in building new concepts about space and astronomy. The freedom for children to spend time internalizing what had been introduced or to extend their knowledge meant that there were no limits for high-achieving children and continual, meaningful reinforcement for low-achieving children. Poetry—from such collections as Livingston's *Sky Songs* (1984), *Earth Songs* (1986), and *Space Songs* (1988); Hopkin's *The Sky Is Full of Song* (1983); and Teasdale's *Stars Tonight* (1930)—was shared across grades, adding to the creative, imaginative quality of the study. When the StarLab was packed away, children were heard making plans for continuing their own star study and predicting what they would confirm when the StarLab came back next year.

REFERENCES

Berman, L., & Fairwell, K. (Eds.). (1988). *Oobleck: What do scientists do?* Great Explorers in Math and Science (GEMS). Berkeley, CA: Lawrence Hall of Science.
Bosworth, D., Geary, P., Johnson, A., Pinkall, J., Probasco, G., & Skinner, R. S. (1979). *The stars and skies project: Activities for the portable planetarium.* ESEA Title IV Project. ESU #11. Holdrege, NE.
Ogle, D. (1986). KWL: A teaching model that develops active reading of expository text. *The Reading Teacher, 39,* 564–570.

CHILDREN'S BOOKS USED IN SCHOOLWIDE STUDY

Adventures of Ranger Rick: Mission to Planet Earth. (1992). *Ranger Rick, 26*(2), 34–37.
Apfel, Necia H. (1991). *Voyager to the planets.* New York: Houghton Mifflin.
Branley, Franklyn M. (1981). *The sky is full of stars.* New York: HarperCollins.
Cole, Joanna. (1990). *The magic school bus lost in the solar system.* Illustrated by Bruce Degen. New York: Scholastic.
D'Aulaire, Ingri, & d'Aulaire, Edgar. (1962). *Book of Greek myths.* New York: Doubleday.
Goble, Paul. (1983). *Star boy.* New York: Bradbury.
Goble, Paul. (1988). *Her seven brothers.* New York: Bradbury.
Green, Timothy. (1991). *Mystery of the Navajo moon.* Flagstaff, AZ: Northland.
Hopkins, Lee Bennett. (1983). *The sky is full of song.* New York: Harper & Row.
Kerrod, Robin. (1988). *Big book of stars and planets.* New York: Smithmark.
Lauber, Patricia. (1990). *Seeing earth from space.* New York: Watts.
Livingston, Myra Cohn. (1984). *Sky songs.* Illustrated by Leonard Fisher. New York: Holiday House.
Livingston, Myra Cohn. (1986). *Earth songs.* Illustrated by Leonard Fisher. New York: Holiday House.
Livingston, Myra Cohn. (1988). *Space songs.* Illustrated by Leonard Fisher. New York: Holiday House.
Mitton, Jacqueline, & Mitton, Simon. (1978). *Concise book of astronomy.* Cambridge, England: Trewin Copplestone.
Moche, Diane. (1975). *What's up there: Questions and answers about stars and space.* New York: Scholastic.

Monjo, Frederick. (1983). *The drinking gourd.* New York: HarperCollins. (Original work published 1970)
Monroe, Jean G., & Williamson, Ray A. (1987). *They dance in the sky: Native American star myths.* Boston: Houghton Mifflin.
Reigot, Betty Polisar. (1988). *A book about planets and stars.* New York: Scholastic.
Schwartz, David. (1985). *How much is a million?* Illustrated by Steven Kellogg. New York: Lothrop, Lee & Shepard.
Simon, Seymour. (1986). *The sun.* New York: Morrow.
Stars. (1988). Voyage Through Universe series. New York: Time-Life Books.
Teasdale, Sara. (1930). *Stars tonight.* New York: Macmillan.
Thompson, C. E. (1989). *Glow in the dark constellations: A field guide for young stargazers.* New York: Putnam.
Udry, Janice. (1959). *The moon jumpers.* Illustrated by Maurice Sendak. New York: HarperCollins.
Yolen, Jane. (1980). *Commander Toad in space.* New York: Putnam.
Yolen, Jane. (1982). *Commander Toad and the planet of grapes.* New York: Putnam.
Yolen, Jane. (1983). *Commander Toad and the big black hole.* New York: Putnam.
Yolen, Jane. (1985). *Commander Toad and the dis-asteroid.* New York: Putnam.
Yolen, Jane. (1986). *Commander Toad and the intergalactic spy.* New York: Putnam.
Yolen, Jane. (1987). *Commander Toad and the space pirates.* New York: Putnam.
Winter, Jane. (1988). *Follow the drinking gourd.* New York: Knopf.

CHILDREN'S BOOKS USED IN GRADE 6

Armbruster, Ann, & Taylor, Elizabeth. (1990). *Astronaut training.* New York: Watts.
Asimov, Isaac. (1988). *Rockets, probes, and satellites.* Milwaukee: Gareth Stevens.
Asimov, Isaac. (1988). *Saturn, the ringed beauty.* Milwaukee: Gareth Stevens.
Asimov, Isaac. (1988). *Uranus, the sideways planet.* Milwaukee: G. Stevens.
Asimov, Isaac. (1989). *Jupiter, the spotted giant.* Milwaukee: Gareth Stevens.
Asimov, Isaac. (1989). *Mercury, quick planet.* Milwaukee: Gareth Stevens.
Asimov, Isaac. (1989). *Mythology and the universe.* Milwaukee: Gareth Stevens.
Asimov, Isaac. (1991). *Colonizing the planets and stars.* New York: Dell.
Asimov, Isaac. (1991). *Comets and meteors.* New York: Dell.
Asimov, Isaac. (1991). *Pluto, a double planet?* New York: Dell.
Behrens, June. (1984). *Sally Ride, astronaut: An American first.* Chicago: Children's Press.
Branley, Franklyn. (1984). *Comets.* New York: HarperCollins
Branley, Franklyn. (1986). *What the moon is like.* New York: HarperCollins.
Branley, Franklyn. (1987). *Planets in our solar system.* New York: HarperCollins.
Branley, Franklyn. (1993). *Sun dogs and shooting stars: A skywatcher's calendar.* New York: Avon.
Brewer, Duncan. (1992). *Comets, asteroids, and meteors.* New York: Marshall Cavendish.

Briggs, Carole S. (1988). *Research balloons: Exploring hidden worlds.* Minneapolis: Lerner.

Briggs, Carole S. (1988). *Women in space: Reaching the last frontier.* Minneapolis: Lerner.

Darling, David. (1987). *Stars: From birth to black holes.* New York: Macmillan.

Embury, Barbara, & Crouch, Tom. (1991). *The dream is alive: A flight of discovery aboard the space shuttle.* New York: HarperCollins.

Fichter, George S. (1982). *Comets and meteors.* New York: Watts.

Furniss, Tim. (1989). *The first men on the moon.* New York: Watts.

Herda, D. J., & Madden, Margaret. (1990). *Operation rescue: Satellite maintenance and repair.* New York: Watts.

Hughes, David. (1989). *The moon.* Planetary Exploration Series. New York: Facts on File.

Jones, Brian. (1993). *The night sky.* Cleveland, OH: Pocket Guide.

Kent, Zachary. (1986). *Story of the Challenger disaster.* Chicago: Children's Press.

Krinov, E., & Romankiewicz, J. (1977). *Giant meteorites.* Elkins Park, PA: Franklin.

Novikov, Isaac. (1990). *Black holes and the universe.* Cambridge, England: Cambridge University Press.

O'Dell, Scott. (1970). *Sing down the moon.* Boston: Houghton Mifflin.

Rey, H. A. (1978). *Find the constellations.* Boston: Houghton Mifflin.

Rickard, Graham. (1989). *Homes in space.* Minneapolis: Lerner.

Sandak, Cass R. (1989). *The world of space.* New York: Watts.

Simon, Seymour. (1979). *Look to the night sky.* New York: Puffin.

Simon, Seymour. (1990). *Uranus.* New York: Morrow.

Simon, Seymour. (1992). *Our solar system.* New York: Morrow.

The sun. (1990). Voyage Through Universe series. New York: Time-Life Books.

Taylor, L. B. (1977). *Gifts from space: How space technology is improving life on earth.* New York: John Day.

Zim, Herbert, & Baker, R. (1985). *Stars: A guide to the constellations.* Racine, WI: Western Publishing.

CHAPTER 6

A Second Chance

At-Risk Students Experience Success
Under a Specialist's Guidance

Nancy DeVries Guth

I enjoy a challenging position in Stafford County, one of the fastest-growing counties in northern Virginia. Our motto is that everyone can and will learn. From central office personnel to teacher, administrator, and parent, we strive to collaborate so that every student can achieve success. As supervisor of reading/language arts and Chapter One reading support programs, my goal is that every student will be provided the additional challenge or extra support necessary to enjoy a successful, literate future. With county support, we provide additional guidance under a reading specialist in each elementary and middle school. We refer to the program as our Reading Support program, and presently employ 14 reading specialists as consultants to the staff and parents. The reading specialists serve as consultants to all teachers and provide recommendations for integrating authentic literature within each classroom curriculum.

Chance was one of the many students in need referred to our Chapter One program. We have designed an eclectic model to accommodate various site, teacher, and student needs. Early intervention for first-graders developing reading and writing confusions is our first priority. Accelerated, intense small-group intervention for second-graders still in the emergent phase of reading is our secondary focus, as is continued contact on a mentor, study-group basis for third- and fourth-graders in need of additional support. The students are seen in small group pull-outs, one-on-one direct tutorial, and in-class team teaching with the classroom teacher and the Chapter One reading specialist. All students in the Chapter-One-served grades have the opportunity to interact with the reading specialist throughout the year. This way, the reading specialist is viewed as reading coach for all the school, students as well as teachers.

In this chapter I highlight the work of Nick Travis, a teacher of young children for 21 years and a reading specialist teaching first in Title One, then in the Chapter One program at many of our county elementary schools. A few years ago Nick was frustrated, as are many teachers, with the lack of interest his students exhibit in learning and class work, and he was getting more bored as each teaching day was marked off the calendar. Yet Nick would enthrall teachers and students alike with the fascinating facts and stories of his summer adventures on dinosaur digs, fossil hunts, and back-packing adventures around the United States. I challenged him to start using material of his choice for teaching. Concerned about his burnout problem, I offered him a proposition: Try teaching from *Ranger Rick*, *National Geographic*, children's own writing, and any other materials he enjoys. I suggested he try it for a year and see if he felt his students made equal or better gains than in the past several years. I trusted him enough as a thoughtful professional to know he would not jeopardize his students by neglecting the skills they needed for success.

He took up the challenge and says his happiest day as a professional was when he burned his dittos and cut up his workbooks to use as scraps for student-created reading and writing journals. Nick relates:

> I used to bore myself by about the third or fourth group of the day. Now I can't wait to get to school each day with the reading material I'd found in my mail or at the library the night before. Teaching has never been so much fun, and in my 20-some years of teaching I've never seen students take off on reading like they do today. I discovered I enjoyed the many big books that are now available, and can teach all the skills my students need by starting with these big books and supplementing with the student's own writing.

His carpeted room now looks like an inviting child's room rather than a classroom, with rocking chairs, bean bags, low apple crates full of books and fossils. In every corner baskets are brimming with books, large pillows are piled by bookshelves, and old cushions surround a tape recorder. Bones and fossils are positioned strategically near complementary reading material, magazines, brochures, and student's "published" writing. His environment is enticing to at-risk students and provides them with a second chance for interaction with learning.

"Wanna hear about tigers?" Chance bounded up to me as soon as I entered the room. He barely waited for an affirmative "Yes" before he scurried to his cubbyhole to pull out his latest manuscript. Proudly he showed me his newest venture, "Tigers."

Nick Travis, his reading coach, came over. "Go ahead, read it to her," he urged. Chance grinned.

"`Tigers,' by Chance," he announced. He continued on to smoothly read descriptions of Sumatran, Siberian, and Bengal tigers, written in approximated spelling typical of a 7-year-old. Skeptically, I asked him if he knew where these tigers would live.

"Sure," he assured me with patient tolerance, "let me show you."

He retrieved a battered classroom globe from the middle of a writing/reading table and proceeded to point out Siberia. "That used to be a part of the Soviet Union," he said, "but it ain't anymore. Mr. Travis told us they all changed their names—but the tigers still live there!" He went on to point out China, India, and even Sumatra with no problem. Still skeptical, I asked him if this was far away from where we live.

"Oh, yeah!" he answered confidently, "we live way over here!" and he showed me the United States, getting as specific as Virginia.

BEGINNING THE YEAR

Quite a different Chance from the reluctant little boy who dragged his feet into Nick's Chapter One room at the beginning of the school year. Chance was one of those tough cases—a virtual nonreader at the beginning of second grade. There was no reason anyone could pinpoint, only lack of practice. Like so many active children, he just was not interested. Consequently, he rarely chose sedentary activities such as reading or writing, and he spent his summer riding bikes, running, and playing rather than sitting down with a book to practice reading.

At one of the first sessions in the fall, I observed how Nick had subtly woven informal assessment throughout the lesson format. When Nick called Chance's group of four, he reluctantly approached the reading table, but his eyes lit up when Nick began the lesson with joking and friendly banter.

"Hey, you ever have Mr. Yuk at your house?" he asked.

"No," all four children responded, looking a little perplexed and shaking their heads questioningly.

"No? We do all the time!" Nick exclaimed. "Especially when I cook! You mean no one ever says 'Yuk' when dinner is served?"

"Yeah." The children got the idea and began to titter as Chance joined in.

"What's the *yuckiest* thing you've ever been served?" queried Nick, tapping into prior knowledge as he linked the known with the lesson.

"Green eggs," a little girl giggled.

"Raw eggs," a young boy offered.

"Brussels sprouts!" another chimed.

"All kinds of eggs," Chance emphatically joined in.

"You don't like eggs?" Nick prodded.

"Nah—they make me throw up!" Chance volunteered with relish.

"Today we're going to read *Yuk Soup* by Joy Cowley (1986c)," Nick said as he pointed to each title word, speaking slowly and deliberately. Chance frowned, but he watched Nick's face and finger carefully.

Nick read several pages, always pointing to the words and drawing attention to the illustrations. At the third or fourth page he asked Chance if he knew what the next word said. Chance looked surprised at himself, yet offered only momentary hesitation as he said "Yuk!"

"Good!" praised Nick. "Now what does it start with?"

After thinking for a moment, Chance responded "*Y*?"

"Great" encouraged Nick, then proceeded to give a minilesson on letter, word, and sound differentiations.

As Nick proceeded to read the entire book, he carefully pointed to every word and involved the students in discussion at almost every page. He often questioned them about the significance of the illustrations, and he constantly pointed out their relationships to the text. Whenever they came to the word "Yuk," all students, including Chance, chimed in.

Nick kept eagle eyes on all the students. As Chance's eyes began to wander, he called him back with his characteristic humor.

"Hey, keep your eyes on me—I'm the cutest guy in the building!" he joked, and Chance would again return his focus to the story page.

At the end of the story, the group was instructed to get their folders. These folders had been previously made by Nick and his students. They consisted of large manila tagboard (9 by 12), taped on three sides and open on one to make a pocket.

The folders were then colorfully decorated with magic markers, personalized by each student as he or she wished. Students began in this way to develop a feeling of literacy ownership, as well as a feeling of belonging in the reading center. All of this groundwork was done by Nick in the first few weeks of school while he was watching faces, eyes, reactions, and responses to books, print, letters, and materials. All this research would be put to use in the daily literacy opportunities, reading and responding to real books, that are the core of his Chapter One program.

Remedial programs, though well-meaning in the past, had focused on having the student do more drill and skill work—more of what had never worked for these learners the first time they were taught the basics of reading and writing. Now, more teachers are realizing that students at risk need better and more books for additional, concentrated contact with print. The specialists in the field of literacy development assist the teacher in making deliberate connections between the text(s), classroom, and everyday life, so the learner makes personal connections. By connecting new information with prior knowledge and past experience, personal literacy grows.

CLASSROOM CONNECTIONS

Nick combines strategies for reading and writing in an interesting, lively presentation every day. He strives to constantly connect the outside world and the child's regular classroom with his reading center. Careful planning and a huge library of interesting child-centered reading material contribute to his goal. Anything in print is game for instruction, whether it be a place mat from McDonald's, a sale catalogue featuring outdoor gear, a stock car magazine, a cookbook—the list is endless. Entering his room is like walking into a treasure chest of print experience. One is literally bathed in print and invited to interact. Books on shelves, books on the floor, books on little tables, even books in the little restroom! And all are coupled with written invitations, such as "Read me if you want to know about animals"; "Read me if you want to find out about habitats." The sign over the door clearly sets the mood for the room: "Parking Zone . . . Readers Only . . . All Others Will Be Towed."

Chance did not see reading as a pleasurable activity when he first entered Nick's room, as one can immediately discern from the reading attitude survey given orally to all students at the beginning of the year. He'd had an enjoyable, active summer and still preferred playing to reading. While Nick was giving Chance the survey, he acted tough and was heard to say he "didn't need this baby stuff," at which time Nick leaned over the table, stared him in the eye, and said "You are mine!" That authoritative voice shocked Chance into quiet observation, and he began to check out other students interacting with the books and reading material laying around the room.

His attitude survey showed that he enjoys checking out books from the library and receiving books as a present, so Nick had a hunch that there was some type of reading material that would interest Chance. He offered a positive comment in regard to using a dictionary. This interesting response informed Nick that Chance enjoyed discovering answers.

When Chance showed that he enjoyed Joy Cowley's *Yuk Soup* (1986c), Nick decided to try *Hungry Monster* (Cowley, 1986b). Chance interacted positively during the group reading and went back to the book several times for rereading on his own, so Nick suggested using the script for a reader's theater. I was privileged to watch the performance and saw Chance struggling to read the lines, but enjoying every minute. He enthusiastically entered in and threw popcorn with gusto as a side effect. By the time they had practiced the play for a full week, they were ready to perform. Chance had memorized his own lines and the lines of others as he practiced. In fact, he had read along quietly with each child as they practiced their parts, and to his surprise he could read the entire book on his own! He was becoming a reader—and it was only Halloween.

Chance's group was invited to perform for his regular second grade class. That was a well-received performance that boosted his self-esteem and established him as a reader in the eyes of his fellow classmates.

After their positive experience with the play, the group begged to perform another. Nick was agreeable, but he challenged the group to write it themselves. Still in the Halloween spirit, they chose the Big Book, *The Secret of Spooky House* (Cowley, 1988). After reading it through several times with Nick as a small group, they each took a little book of the story and decided who would play each part. Chance was determined to be a part of all scenes and readily assumed his part with enthusiasm. They performed the play several times before Thanksgiving break for various school audiences and were much congratulated. The principal was delighted to attend a performance and praised their efforts highly. She had been an enthusiastic supporter of Nick's program as he made the transition to real books and contributed supplementary funds whenever possible.

In October Chance had struggled through *Hungry Monster* for his independent silent reading. Since he enjoyed the book and was developing some confidence as a strategic reader, Nick suggested *Kick-a-Lot Shoes* (1987a) by the same author. He spent two weeks in November with the book and returned from Thanksgiving vacation feeling confident and ready to read. His supportive mother was thrilled with his progress and began taking him to the public library. Nick assured her that more difficult informational books were great for him to check out for practice, as the easier books at his level of independent reading often did not appeal to him.

On December 2 Chance made history as a developing reader. He asked to check out *two* books for independent reading—*Houses* (Cowley, 1986a) and *Underwater Journey* (Cutting, 1990)! These were in response to the regular classroom theme of habitat—for people and animals. Chance was beginning to see reading as a way to find out information and a valuable option even for tough guys. The themes taught in the classroom were reinforced by Nick's work with his students through vivid informational books on similar topics. The children always wanted to be as close to him as possible while he was showing them how to get information from books (see Figure 6.1).

FIGURE 6.1. Nick Travis assists some of his reading center students as they explore curricular material.

Then came Christmas, and Nick wondered if Chance would lose his zeal for reading over the holidays. In contrast, Chance returned with renewed vigor for discovering new answers to his endless curiosity. He brought in pamphlets from a visit over Christmas to the Smithsonian Museum of Natural History and brimming with information about his trip to the nearby Washington Zoo. This development fit perfectly as a supplement to the study of animals and habitats, the ongoing classroom theme.

DIRECTED VIEWING

Nick works to develop prior knowledge for his at-risk students before classroom themes are introduced. He is an avid watcher of the Discovery channel as well as any other educational television features. He constantly tapes appropriate shows and incorporates them into his classroom lessons.

When used wisely, videos can be an excellent source for developing prior knowledge, expanding vocabulary, and igniting one's curiosity about a subject. Nick often plugs into upcoming classroom themes by using videos to develop a knowledge base for his students. This provides the students with the confidence they need to participate in classroom discussions and reading assignments. The reading center student then can predict unknown words with some degree of certainty, and after Nick's guided assistance often becomes the classroom expert.

The study of animals and habitats is a standard curriculum objective for second-graders. A video from National Geographic on endangered species is a stimulating introduction to the study as Nick orchestrates it. This ensures a common vocabulary from which to begin. As the students illustrate vocabulary words from the video, they practice visualization skills and begin their glossary. (Textbooks are also excellent resources when used with discretion.) After the video, students naturally begin to ask questions, and they are guided first to textbooks to find answers. Nick makes use of textbooks from previous adoption cycles as well as older versions no longer in use from his reference shelves. With older students he requires that they bring their classroom texts with them, or he works in their classroom team-teaching with their teacher. We have found small-group sessions to be more beneficial with students who are in need of intense, accelerated intervention. With this method they often achieve a reading and writing competency equal to that of the average of the class within one school year.

GUIDED RESEARCH

Many sessions in the reading center are devoted to how to read a content-area text. Nick zeros in on teaching concepts such as looking for the dark print, the headings under which you find information on that topic. He follows with practice in observation of each photograph and picture and reading the captions underneath, then asking what they have learned from the pictures. The next step is to read the small introduction at the beginning of the chapter (asking "What am I going to learn?") and then move to the summary at the end of the chapter (asking "What should I remember?") before going over the questions at the end of the chapter. The questions give direction to what topics demand concentration in the chapter reading.

Chance looked worried when Nick brought out the textbooks, but his curiosity got the best of him, and he was beginning to think of himself as a reader since his experience with performing the play. He found himself intently checking out the print to find answers to his questions. Nick provided support for predicting words, explaining phrases, and guiding comprehension. Interest prevailed, and to his surprise Chance found himself calling to his fellow group members to exclaim over tiger and habitat facts! Quite a different little guy from the too tough nonreader I had observed several months before.

After Chance was comfortable with the textbook reading, he was ready to join the others in writing response. The students were guided into taking notes. Categories of information were suggested by the group, and the headings were written in large print on chart paper:

What they look like
Where they live
What they eat
Who their enemies are

As the students read their chosen books, magazines, and articles, they constantly referred to the chart. This would trigger their memory on what information to record. Nick was actively circulating, and often two or more of the group would be calling to him with questions, concerns, or excitement.

In addition to the categories having been listed on the chart, students put each as a heading on the top of a page of their writing journal. In this way they learned the skill of strategic note taking. Children with few literacy encounters often have a very difficult time organizing information. They have the ability to take notes, but freeze because they do not know where to put this information. When provided with a schema with which to organize material, they are enabled to take notes with pride and participate as an equal classroom learner. Chance stumbled over many words, but like so many unpracticed readers, he learned words that interested him quickly. He was able to predict words by using the visuals provided in the books and was able to recall the words in phrases the following day. After two weeks of note taking, he could readily read all his notes and elaborate on the copied information.

The next two weeks were spent with each student writing a report and illustrating it (see Figure 6.2). Illustrations were labored over to achieve correct dimensions and accurate coloring. Even through drawing, Nick emphasized reading carefully to see if the description in their reports matched the appearance in their drawings.

The final product was commendable for any second-grader. The reports were carefully printed, neatly spaced, and well organized. Visuals were brightly colored and placed complementarily to the text. The cover

FIGURE 6.2. Nick Travis oversees Chance illustrating his report.

was decorated construction paper, the binding only stapled, but it looked great! The students were so proud—and felt the reports were something they could do themselves at home or in their regular class. They were on the road to becoming independent, lifelong learners.

Nick never hurried his students, yet never allowed their attention to wander or anyone to sit idle. He encouraged every effort with lavish praise, thus developing active, eager learners. After their positive experience with this report, the students were eager to continue with another. The topic coordinated with topics being discussed in the regular classroom, so they were asked to give their reports to the class. In this way the classroom study was enhanced by the reading and writing from the Chapter One room, and the students felt themselves on equal-learner status with the rest of the class.

CREATIVE COLLABORATIONS

Literacy cannot be the responsibility of one person or even several people in each school building. Just as an African proverb states that it takes a whole village to educate a child, so it takes the coordinated efforts of an entire school district. The school board, central office, administrators, teachers, parents, and students contribute to the literacy demands needed in our society. Collaboration on a professional level is essential if a teacher or specialist is going to be truly effective and not become exhausted or disillusioned. All personnel can contribute from their areas of expertise and from their hobbies, such as Nick's passion for science. In our school district, Nick has become the specialist on interactive science. Every elementary school now gives him a call during their dinosaur studies, and he visits the school with his fossils, entertaining stories, and a bag full of books, pamphlets, magazines, and brochures. He stages geology hunts by burying fossils and bones during the earth science studies, and comes with his star-gazing telescope and star tent for study of the solar system. Another teacher contributes her rain-forest-transformed classroom, another her study of artists, and the school's curriculum is enriched in an effective, memory-producing manner. When collaboration becomes the curriculum model, teachers nurture one another and develop the potential stored in the treasure of their expertise.

Connecting concepts into creative curriculum produces a deeper level of learning, as well as ownership for the learner. As concepts are reinforced and complemented through a variety of contexts—including reading, writing, social studies, science, health, and art—the possibilities are endless. The ideas take on greater significance for the students, and school becomes more like real-life experiences. Literature is the thread that can unite the subject areas and become an integral part of the learner's life, both in school and outside the formal school situation. Our county's reading program is called TAPS: teachers, administrators, parents, and students tapping into real literature. The ageless power of real literature touches all learners, from the gifted to the less academically able, and in response to the literature, their personal literacy flourishes. The countywide special reading program includes guidelines for collaboration with parents, students, and classroom teachers (see Figure 6.3).

A year later Chance is still drawn to Nick's room. He comes to share his latest experiences as a reader and as a friend. They chat about weekend activities, discuss their latest exploring adventures, and share recommendations for books, magazines, and other reading materials. He no longer is formally listed as a Chapter One student because he is reading as well as his grade-level peers, yet he still voluntarily seeks out the support of a friendly professional.

Friendly, nonjudgmental professional support is just as necessary for

FIGURE 6.3. Guidelines for collaboration in Stafford County's special reading program

Stafford County Special Reading Program		
Parents	**Students**	**Teachers**
Be involved in modeling self-initiated reading and writing	Become motivated for independent reading and writing	Work with parents and reading specialist to develop individual literacy plans for each student
Learn child's strengths to help him/her overcome difficulties	Understand the positive relationship between reading time and growth of proficiency	Conference with parents, students, and specialist to keep all informed on student's progress
Participate actively in child's classroom and/ or parent workshop on occasional evenings	Receive individual or small group direct instruction as needed	Obtain materials appropriate for the student's interest and ability level
	Enjoy their status as successful classroom participants	

teacher growth as student growth. Exchanging ideas, sharing books, and natural dialogue about projects that exceeded expectations are essential for a sense of excitement and renewal for all professionals.

CHILDREN'S BOOKS

Braus, J., Allman, J., Marshal, V., & Hitchner, V. (1991). *Amazing animals: Question and answer book*. Montreal: Tarmani.
Brockman, Alfred. (1986). *Lions and tigers*. Windmere, FL: Rourke Enterprises.
Chipperfield, M. (1977). *Lions*. Windmere, FL: Rourke Enterprises.
Cowley, J. (1986a) *Houses*. Bothell, WA: Wright Group.
Cowley, J. (1986b). *Hungry monster*. Bothell, WA: Wright Group.
Cowley, J. (1986c). *Yuk soup*. Bothell, WA: Wright Group.
Cowley, J. (1987a). *Kick-a-lot shoes*. Bothell, WA: Wright Group.
Cowley, J. (1987b). *The terrible tiger*. Bothell, WA: Wright Group.

Cowley, J. (1988). *The Secret of the Spooky House*. Bothell, WA: Wright Group.

Cutting, B. (1990). *Underwater journey*. Bothell, WA: Wright Group.

Graham, T. (1983). *The tiger*. Windmere, FL: Rourke Enterprises.

Graver, E. (1968). *The cats*. New York: Time-Life Films.

Green, Carl. (1986). *The Bengal tiger*. Mankato, MN: Baker St. Products.

Greer, A. (1994). *Tigers*. San Diego, CA: Wildlife (Zoobooks).

Gregory, O. B. (1982). *The big cats*. Windmere, FL: Rourke Enterprises.

Hoffman, Mary. (1984). *Tiger*. Milwaukee, WI: Raintree Books.

Nentl, Jerolyn. (1984). *The wild cats*. Mankato, MN: Crestwood House.

CHAPTER 7

Using Real Literature in a Multi-Age Setting

How to Survive Spring

Marilyn Thompson

This chapter describes an example of successful collaborations in a school community. It demonstrates how a curricular unit can be built around information already present in a multi-age setting or regular classroom and extended to new learning. In this study of gardening, Marilyn Thompson, the reading specialist, reports on collaboration that occurred naturally between the students of various ages, the classroom teachers, other school specialists, and community members. The study described is from a multi-age school setting and is an example of constructing a curricular study around the students' prior knowledge of gardening and developing the study to include new skills and ideas.

The study built around the garden is an example of cross-curricular integration that developed naturally from the community interests and the learning goals of the teacher. The prior knowledge that students bring with them is used as the foundation. Authentic literature is incorporated with textbook facts and life experiences. Reading, writing, scientific data collections, graphing, mapping, and many other curricular objectives are taught with the perspective and voice of an enthusiastic author. When curriculum objectives are taught with real-life activities, students attach meaning to the learning and it becomes real for them. As students see connections between the life of the classroom and the life of their homes, books assume a personal meaning and are eagerly carried home to share with family and friends.

The Primary I (kindergarten/first grade) classes and Primary II (second/third grade) classes collaborated naturally throughout all phases of this study. They modeled researching, recording, even hoeing and raking techniques for the less familiar. No attention was paid to the age of the learner. This study poignantly illustrated that the amount of prior exposure and experience with a topic or task was the determiner to the level of proficiency, not age or probable intelligence.

Everyone's many intelligences were celebrated throughout this study. Since many of Marilyn's students are kinesthetic learners, they excelled at this opportunity to actively participate in real-life, hands-on activities. Family members who previously had been reluctant to participate in school studies now felt comfortable sharing their knowledge of gardening. Grandparents, younger brothers and sisters, mothers and fathers all became actively involved, as they felt they had some ability or knowledge to contribute. It was a community collaboration, building curriculum for the life of the learner. This study could easily be taught in any classroom and community, as many levels of learning and expertise exist in every setting.

Hartwood Elementary School, where I teach, is located 50 miles south of Washington, DC, and 50 miles north of Richmond, Virginia. The atmosphere and social climate are as equidistant between these extremes as the location. In our school of approximately 600 students in kindergarten through grade 5, we have children of farmers whose families have lived in Hartwood for generations and children of upwardly mobile professionals who work in Washington, as well as many children of the military from the Quantico Marine base. Two years ago, Hartwood applied for and received a Restructuring Early Childhood Education grant from the state of Virginia. As part of our restructuring program, during the 1993–1994 school year, our primary children have been grouped in Primary I (which replaced kindergarten and first grade) or Primary II (which replaced the second and third grades). Several children have moved back and forth between the two. Both our Chapter One program and our special education program are based on the inclusion model. This means the children are serviced within the regular classroom rather than pulled out. Our speech therapist works closely with the classroom teachers to develop activities that are connected to the curriculum, so that all our instruction is related, and none occurs in isolation. All our classes are heterogeneously grouped.

In my position as the Chapter One reading specialist, I have had the unique opportunity to participate in most of the Primary I and Primary II classes. We use trade books, poems, songs, stories, and plays to teach all the language arts, and we occasionally supplement with basal readers. We don't believe any aspect of children's learning—whether it be math concepts, beginning sounds, or problem solving—occurs in isolation. Rather, we teach the whole child from a developmental perspective. This year we have had many visitors. We have learned many things about teachers as well as teaching. The most critical thing in teaching that is effective and developmentally appropriate is that the philosophy of the teacher match his or her practices. We are convinced that the reason many people fail at teaching whole language is that they don't really believe it reflects the way children learn. They use the ideas they find in teacher books, but they don't know how to fix an idea that doesn't work, or how to adapt it to their own style. To be an effective teacher is to teach the way you believe children learn best.

THE GARDEN

My favorite theme, and the one that makes May tolerable, is "The Garden." This is a theme that has been used successfully in Primary I and Primary II and can be used every year, even in a multi-age classroom where the same children stay for two years. Through our investigation into developmentally appropriate curriculum for young children, we heard of a program in which each grade level planted a garden that had a connection to a certain book. For instance, young children planted a garden modeled after "Mr. McGregor's" in *The Tale of Peter Rabbit* (Potter, 1902/ 1972) and older children had a "Secret Garden" (Burnett, 1910/1989). We loved this idea but felt we should modify it to our own particular community. Our idea was even more ambitious than the original. In the 1992–1993 school year two classes tilled (by hand) the very hard Virginia clay and worked together to grow vegetables and flowers. This was a cooperative project between a first-grade and a third-grade class, although each class had their own garden. The third-graders did the original research and planted a replica of a World War II victory garden. The first-graders consulted the third-graders as experts when they were ready to plant a flower garden. The teachers and I worked together to find appropriate books, poems, and songs.

Michele Solomon, who taught the third-grade gardeners, provided an outline for her multi-age team to follow in 1993–1994. I will describe her modified plan.

Before beginning any of the activities below, she conducts a KWL (Ogle, 1986), whereby children are surveyed to see how much they already *know* about gardens (K) and what they *want* to learn (W). The L comes later, when the children report what they have *learned*. This KWL is a very important step. Many of the Chapter One and other "at-risk" children have a great deal of knowledge in these areas. Getting at this information in advance will greatly enhance their chances for success. How much the children know already will, of course, determine how much of the information below a teacher would be able to cover.

The next step is to begin soil research. The objective is to determine what is the best possible type of soil to use in the growing of vegetables. The Activities to Integrate Mathematics and Science (AIMS) guide, *Overhead and Underfoot*, has several good experiments, such as "What makes soil?" (Wiebe, 1987, pp. 46–47). The grade-level science text or those for other grade levels may have some appropriate material. The State Cooperative Extension Service provides this type of information free to farmers of any age. When the proper soil is determined, discussions focus on how composting can enhance soil for the garden, and composting experiments begin. What rots, how fast, and under what conditions? Another excellent source is *Exploring the World of Plants and Soils* (1993). This is a pamphlet that is used as the "beginner member's manual" and is published by the National 4-H Council. It is filled with experiments and ideas. The gardening section of the local public library should be checked for both adult and juvenile materials.

After soil experiments are completed and conclusions drawn, Michele begins discussions and experiments on the nature of plants. What parts do they have? How do they survive? What elements are necessary for their survival? The MECC computer program, "Wooly's Garden" (1993), which is available for Apple II, allows young aspiring gardeners to manipulate light, water, and other variables and compare yields. Wooly keeps a journal, where he records all his data. This is a great model for the children and is readable by almost all second- and third-graders. Again, the science text may provide a wealth of information. The book *The Reason for a Flower* (Heller, 1993) is also helpful for figuring out the nature of plants. *Exploring the World of Plants and Soils* (1993) will be an asset here, too. Experiments that use full-grown seedlings make it possible for children to observe directly the consequences of too much or too little light or water. Experiments based on children's ideas are important. They might want to know if plants need soil. After they have experimented and made discoveries, a discussion and research of hydroponics, growing plants in water, might be in order.

In the next step, discussions begin about actual kinds and species of plants. The children do lots of KWL-type activities, coupled with sorting and classifying, to narrow plant species into different groups. Several days' worth of activities are planned to break plants into groups based on the following characteristics: How do they grow—bush, small plant, tree, shrub, vine, or root? What type of seed do they produce—fruit, root, nut, and so forth? What are they used for—medicine, eating, decoration, and so forth?

Which ones should be included in a garden? This will require information on growing times, space needed, and companion plants. These activities are imperative in order for the children to be able to make connections later on when they are designing the actual garden scheme. They will need to know that cucumbers grow on a vine and that corn is a stalk. They should be able to infer later that the two can be planted in the same mound based on their characteristics.

When the children have finished their study of plant characteristics, they are ready to move on to garden planning. As a group, they select what vegetables to include in the garden. This is the actual hands-on planning phase. The children select a variety of vegetables, such as lettuce, radishes, onions, turnips, spinach, broccoli, cauliflower, beets, corn, squash, watermelons, beans, peas, and so forth. Then, as a group, they narrow the choices down into workable solutions based on practical conditions, such as space available. Once the decisions have been made on what to plant, the real research activities begin. At this point, copies of gardening books, magazines, seed catalogues, and pamphlets fill the classroom.

The children usually work best in cooperative learning groups of two. They pick a vegetable to research. They will need to read and learn about

Planting times, zones, and last expected frost
How long the seeds take to germinate
Whether the seeds need to be planted inside first
Whether they should be planted in mounds, rows, or beds
How the plant grows—straight up, sideways, spreads, or roots
Distances needed between plants
Whether successive plantings are needed
How to thin the seedlings
Companion herbs or vegetables to consider
The natural enemies of the plants

Once this information is gathered, it is shared with the class through discussions and project presentations. A plan of action for the actual planting of the garden is developed, based on the children's research and conclusions. There are some very easy books, such as *Pumpkin, Pumpkin* (Titherington, 1986), that do not provide much content but are an excellent starting point for some children. Although there are no statistics on growing times, the cycle from seed to fruit is covered and illustrated quite well in some books. This type of book is primarily informational but may also contain a story or have lovely illustrations. This type of book is perfect to raise and maintain the children's interest level (such as *Planting a Rainbow* [Ehlert, 1988]).

It is also during this stage that the physical preparation for the garden begins. Tilling, raking, and, in Virginia, removing rocks take large amounts of time. Another alternative is to enlist the aid of parent volunteers who are willing to donate their time and the dirt and materials necessary for raised beds. These, which look like giant sandboxes, can be used again and again, in either a rural or suburban setting.

Finally, planting and observing the plants in the garden begin. The raised beds make it easier for young children to prepare the soil for the planting (see Figure 7.1). More research can follow after the garden has been planted. Now is a good time to delve into activities such as the following:

> Container gardening
> Investigating helpful creatures such as worms, toads, and ladybugs
> Reading many fiction and nonfiction books about gardening
> Sharing expertise with other grade levels through presentations and
>   project sharing
> Daily garden observation and tending
> Writing garden poetry (the cinquain form lends itself very well to
>   nonfiction topics and the kids like the structure)
> Publishing gardening posters and fact books

Big Books about fruits and vegetables are wonderful to share at this stage. The children love to read and reread them, and even the older children really like this format.

The culminating activity is the harvesting. Hopefully the young gardeners have chosen some plants that have a short enough growing time that some of the products are ready to eat by the end of the year. Radishes, lettuce, and beans grow quite quickly. If possible, the classroom collaborates with the summer school teachers to extend the project and the harvesting.

READING AND WRITING CONNECTIONS

One of the most useful tools in this study is the theme logs the students develop over the course of the unit. All observations, research, pictures, and related assignments are recorded in this log, which can be used as a reference by the children and as an assessment tool by the teacher. This is an excellent way to teach skills of data collection and note taking. Several other types of reading and writing are also encouraged during this unit. Kris wrote her teacher about her white oak:

FIGURE 7.1. Raised bed gardens constructed with the collaborative efforts of parents, teachers, and students

Dear Mrs. Solomon,

Yesterday we planted White Oak trees. Kainoa's is dead, he planted it in clay. Brandon Travis and I planted are's together by a large White Oak. The soil was very rich in nutrants and castings, yumy for worms. The large White oak will help it because when the White oak falls it will decompose and make very rich soil! Are trees will help each other because they can hook on to each other and form a couple huge roots to crawl to the center of the earth, and get more water.

Kris Warren, Grade 3

As described earlier, the children need to research insects, soil conditions, composting, worms, and growing conditions. There are many excellent nonfiction sources available to children. We always look for books with an index and a table of contents. Many beginning reference books omit these two essentials. Seed packets and gardening catalogues provide a wealth of information that is generally not too difficult to read and is often accompanied by graphs. There are several good children's gardening books that have been published recently, as well as adult how-to books. After the student groups begin sharing their research with the entire class, their projects, notes, and "published" books become a source of information for the other children. The student-generated texts are often more readable. Graphing appropriate information such as growing times, as the children collect it, is another way to create and provide accessible reference sources.

The children use real text in many ways during this study. The older children are able to research what plants will grow well in this area. They can investigate such areas as companion plants, natural pest control, and water and space requirements using many different resources. They read gardening catalogues, seed packets, encyclopedias, almanacs, and history books, use reference materials on compact discs, and call the Smithsonian Institution(s) and the Cooperative Extension Service. If they decide to make a theme garden, such as the World War II victory garden or one connected to a book, they need to do the appropriate research to guarantee authenticity. If they decide to make raised-bed gardens, the children have to do extensive research into the types of wood they should use, and how much and what kind of soil they should get in addition to all the activities above.

After the children have done the research, they are ready to plant. Each team of two children who work together to research a specific plant make a row marker for it, including lots of information about the plant and a picture. It is a real joy for the Chapter One children and other young beginning readers to identify the plants by reading the markers and watching them grow. The gardeners also make a large laminated sign describing the garden, especially if it is a theme garden such as a victory garden. The younger readers really enjoy reading and rereading this.

For several weeks during this unit—both in the classroom and as Chapter One, speech, and special education enrichment—we use stories related to plants, flowers, and gardens as our reading material. In both multi-age and single-grade classes, the children complete reading contracts that have similar elements. Children always record certain information— title, author, and date—and are encouraged to respond in writing to what they have read in a reading journal. They usually read their books, or at least a portion, more than once to develop fluency. When they are spending a lot of energy and time on a subject, they have a tendency to want to read books about it, too. Since they are often reading more than one, and each child may have a different book, it is essential to have many, many books on a theme. We raid the local library as well as the school library. We have also purchased several related book sets. It is particularly important to have books at different readability levels. Tilling the ground makes the children want to read about other children who have done the same. They need access to books that are at their instructional and independent reading level.

LEARNING TOGETHER

Over the two years of our gardening experiences we discovered both ex-pected and unexpected benefits. One of the great advantages of conduct-ing this study in a multi-age setting is that the children stay with the same teacher, and hence the same garden, for two years. Designing and start-ing projects and experiments is much easier in a multi-age classroom. Skeptical second-graders who tended to think that things were impossible to find out and had a hard time starting projects thrived when exposed to the enthusiasm of the older children, who were often the catalyst they needed to get moving. Our weather is such that there should be a few things like pumpkins ready to harvest in the fall. This continuity is great for developing a sense of belonging in the children, who talk about com-ing back to school with anticipation. We found a great surge of commu-nity help and parent volunteerism. Last year, since the garden was near the road, the local community kept it harvested. This year we had many parents, children, and teachers work together on an April weekend to build and fill the raised beds. There were some parents, especially fathers, who had never volunteered at school before but who seemed very comfort-able with this project and were enthusiastically willing to help. Four Pri-mary II classes planted raised bed gardens this year (see Figure 7.2). This would have been impossible without the support of the parents. Probably the most valuable lesson we all learned was that we did not have to do all the planning by ourselves. The specialists in speech, reading, music, physi-cal education, and art, the librarian, and the classroom teachers worked together with each other and with the parents to plan activities. The chil-dren themselves often provided the direction for the studies through their curiosity and willingness to learn.

What we discovered through our learning process is that the best themes for integrated study, those which contain the most learning po-tential, are those which reflect the children's interests and community. For instance, three years ago, as a second-grade teacher, I hatched chick-ens, geese, and quail in the classroom. The children immersed themselves in books about birds. They made graphs of turning times and hatching dates. They read and wrote constantly about birds. In retrospect this unit was successful because, like the garden unit, it allowed the children to fully

FIGURE 7.2. Kainoa prepares the ground for planting in the raised bed garden.

engage all their senses, and involved the whole child in something that he or she considered important. They were able to touch, hear, smell, and wait for the baby birds to be born. In a coastal school, the ocean is probably a good choice for a unit, but living in a rural setting as we do, children have a hard time conceptualizing the vastness of the sea and what it contains.

We have had a wonderful time planting our gardens and singing our garden songs, and the children have learned more than we thought possible. In the coming years we are considering a greenhouse and a vegetable stand. The garden theme is one with many variations. When designed as a spring event, the garden theme can be naturally carried over into the summer school curriculum, extending collaborative relationships and curricular connections. The possibilities are as limitless as the imagination and interests of the children and their teachers.

REFERENCES

Ogle, D. (1986). KWL: A teaching model that develops active reading of expository text. *The Reading Teacher*, 39, 564–570.

Wiebe, A. J. (1987). *Overhead and underfoot*. Fresno, CA: AIMS Educational Foundation.

CHILDREN'S BOOKS

Burnett, Frances H. (1989). *The secret garden*. New York: Viking. (Original work published 1910)
Ehlert, Lois. (1988). *Planting a rainbow*. New York: Harcourt Brace.
Exploring the world of plants and soils. (1993). Washington, DC: National 4-H Foundation.
Heller, Ruth. (1993). *The reason for a flower*. New York: Grosset & Dunlap.
Potter, Beatrix. (1972). *The tale of Peter Rabbit*. New York: Warne. (Original work published 1902)
Titherington, Jeanne. (1986). *Pumpkin, pumpkin*. New York: Greenwillow.

CHAPTER 8

Building Bridges

Norma Boehm

Norma Boehm, a dynamic fifth-grade teacher at Creston Christian School in
Grand Rapids, Michigan, has always taught using thematic units and
emphasizing writing. She has a sign above her desk that states *I came to
teach, but I stayed to learn.*

Recently, her continued study of how children learn, and her work as
teacher consultant and researcher with the Michigan State University Red
Cedar Writing Project, led her to a more complete integration of her
curriculum. In this chapter, Norma tells us how she chose Bridges as a topic
for a year-long study relating concepts, skills, and attitudes. Right from the
beginning the students made personal connections, continually integrating
their new information and ideas with prior knowledge and past experiences.

After recounting the planning process, she shares some of the highlights
of various segments of the integrated study. The students were actively
engaged in decision making, and flexibility in scheduling and planning was
apparent. Norma weaves *choice* into all of her teaching. The fifth-graders
helped plan the visits with the elderly, their own reading, and their research
topic. They took charge of their bridge-building company and chose their
own jobs for the building project.

To Norma, all of teaching is collaboration. Each year she welcomes a
student teacher or intern from a local college into her classroom as a
professional partner. The two confer and learn from each other and from
the fifth-graders. She cooperates wholeheartedly with fellow teachers who
propose joint projects and works closely with the school librarian. In this
study she reaches out into the community for further collaboration.

Beginning a new school year always generates mixed feelings in my
teacher soul. I look forward with anticipation to new faces and experiences,
wondering what I will learn, but I feel a great deal of apprehension about

the nature of the new students with whom I will work. What are their interests? What are their needs? Will they work well together as a group? Will they initiate questions to fuel our learning or will they depend on me? I wrestle with these questions and others every year as I attempt to create a climate of discovery in our community of learners. I'd like to take you on a journey through one year, documenting my first attempt at connecting learning through a year-long theme by collaboration with students, colleagues, and the community.

LAYING THE FOUNDATION

The students left for home and the last toothpick was swept from the floor. My student teacher and I sat down to reflect on what had happened during the last two weeks as she worked with our fifth-graders on a prepared integrated unit, *Building Toothpick Bridges* (Pollard, 1985). The engagement, collaboration, and learning had been exceptional for the last two weeks of the school year. The final day seemed to come too soon. What was there about this experience that so effectively captured the attention of the students? Several answers came to mind: learning about the structure of a bridge, planning and building with a group, drawing a blueprint, negotiating a budget, and the competition on bridge-breaking day to see which group had designed the strongest bridge.

Bridges . . . where would a topic like that take us? How could we extend this experience? Our minds began to race and I felt like I had been launched into the coming year—a "bridge" stretching from June to September! I began to think about ways that a single theme could provide us with a way of looking at many areas of life and learning, and I recorded my ideas in the form of a web. The flexibility, open-endedness, and connecting possibilities of "bridges" excited me, along with the fact that I knew so little about them, confirming my status as an authentic learner along with my students.

Designing a Plan

My next step was to begin a "to-do" list. Although I intended to follow my students' lead, I knew I would have to spark their interest in bridges and then be aware of specific ways I could assist their search for information. My beginning list looked like this:

1. Find four or five informational books on bridges and purchase multiple copies for reading response groups (types of bridges, bridge construction, bridges in Michigan and in the United States, history of bridges).

2. Find four or five novels depicting bridges in relationships (friends, countries, cultures, special needs, divorce, death, childhood/adolescence) and
   purchase multiple copies for reading response groups.
3. Shop for posters of bridges.
4. Call the department of transportation to locate someone (who likes
   children and bridges) to meet us at the oldest and newest bridges in
   Grand Rapids and answer our questions.
5. Locate an architect who has designed a bridge to come to school and
   show us the process.
6. Write and send a letter to my prospective students in August to initiate
   thinking about bridges.

Collaborating with Colleagues and Students

The first thing I did in August was to purchase a book called *Travels Across
the Curriculum: Models for Interdisciplinary Learning* (Tchudi, 1991). It was a
quick read, gave a foundation to my ideas, and proved to be a valuable
resource, applicable from elementary through college.

Next, I prepared a letter and reflection paper for my new students. I
wanted them to begin thinking about bridges well before they entered our
classroom.

> Dear ———,
>
> It's only a short time until we begin a new school year to-
> gether. I look forward to getting to know you and to the things we
> will learn. I would like to invite you to join me in preparation for
> our first day.
>
> I have enclosed a reflection paper for you. This will help me
> get to know about your talents and interests inside and outside of
> school. Please take your time with this paper. I encourage you to
> discuss it with your parents, but I'd like the written reflection to be
> your work. You may mail it to me, drop it off if you come by school
> to visit, or take it with you the first day of school [see Figure 8.1].
>
> Secondly, I have chosen a theme of *Bridges*. I hope this will
> help connect our learning in all subject areas. Would you do some
> thinking about the topic of bridges before our first day? Please read
> the list below and either choose one item to do as your "before-
> school-starts-project" or come up with an idea on your own. We
> will meet in small groups the first day to talk about what we did.
> Here is the list, but remember, you may think of something you
> would enjoy more!

1. Look up the word *bridge* in the dictionary and write down the definition.
2. Look up *bridge* in the encyclopedia and jot down a few interesting facts.
3. Bring in a photo of a bridge with its name and location.
4. Design and draw or build a model of a bridge of your own.
5. Brainstorm a list of other things in life that serve as bridges from one person to another, such as an apology to a friend whose feelings you have hurt.
6. Write a few sentences about someone or something in the Bible that served as a bridge between God and man.
7. Write a poem (it doesn't have to rhyme!)
8. Sit by a bridge near your home and write a short piece either describing the structure itself or observing the purpose of the bridge and the resulting activity on or under it.

It will be fun to share what we have discovered or created when we get together on our first day of school.

Sincerely,
Norma Boehm

Many students stopped by before our first day of school to give me their reflections and add their bridge projects to the classroom display. They brought dictionary definitions, an electronic encyclopedia entry, photographs from their vacations, drawings, and a diorama.

When I went shopping for posters of bridges, I found an inexpensive and generous supply at our local grocery/department store. On a weekend trip to the Mackinac Bridge, our principal bought me a beautiful poster of our famous Michigan landmark. Our room definitely began to take on a bridge motif. A meeting with our librarian resulted in the purchase of several books about bridges to be added to our media center collection.

And then, I had a wonderful surprise! A teacher friend, Dave Vermeulen, was returning to our second grade after spending a year teaching in Rehoboth, New Mexico, where he had collaborated with a fifth-grade teacher. He asked if my students and I would like to be involved in a three-way partnership—fifth-graders, second-graders, and nursing home residents. I was so excited! This was an opportunity to build bridges to younger students and to the elderly. Where would this lead us academically?

FIGURE 8.1. Brad's August reflection

August
REFLECTIONS OF

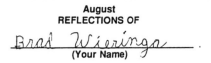
(Your Name)

1. **As I look back over the summer, these are the things I spent quite a bit of time doing:** did some models, I took a computer class at CC (Community college) I took art classes at Kendall College of Art and Design.

2. **I think I am pretty good at:**

    Mathematics, Reading, Computers.

3. **Activities I participate in outside of school are:**

    Base Ball, Cadets, fishing, doodling.

4. **I really like it when my teacher:**

    is usually in a good mood.

5. **It bothers me a lot when my teacher:**

    confuses me with other students

6. **I hope that in my classroom we:**

    participate in fun math games.

7. **Some things I like to read and learn about are:** I like to read Long science fiction books (for instance I'm reading Consider Phlebas, 495 pages.) I like to learn about space and science.

8. **One goal I'd like to set for myself in school this year is:**

    To improve my artistic talents in art class.

Reading About Structural Bridges

As the students entered the first day, they added their bridge projects to the bulletin board. We spent time talking about what they brought and made a web on the chalkboard of things we already knew about bridges, which was not very much! In small groups, we generated lists of questions for which we wanted to find answers. They included questions about history, what bridges are made of, what makes a bridge strong, and questions about specific famous bridges. I had all our media center bridge books (see Children's Books at the end of the chapter) lined up on the chalk ledge and briefly introduced each one. During the next three weeks I expected each person to read *How We Build Bridges* (Ardley, 1990) and at least three other books about bridges. Findings were to be recorded in their reading response journals. This provided us with some common knowledge and language.

Helping the Second-Graders

When we knew our weekly schedules, Dave and I met to arrange a time when our classes could meet daily. Both Dave and I teach spelling with some individualization. We begin each week with some content words or words that follow a spelling pattern, but many words are taken from each student's writing. This was where the second-graders needed us most at the beginning of the year. Every day right after recess we joined them for about 20 minutes. We helped the second-graders make their word lists, talked about the spelling of the words, gave them pretests and final tests. Our help was also needed to sign out classroom books to each student for evening reading. Once a week, the partners read together for 20 minutes. Back in our home classroom we had many talks about how to teach without just telling. We talked about problems with cooperation and attitude. It gave us a purposeful opportunity to examine our own processes of learning and share ideas of alternate methods to be used with our second-grade partners.

SPANNING GENERATIONS

To begin our work with Rest Haven, Dave and I met with Kim Murphy, the activities director. We spent a long time carefully matching our student partners with a compatible "grandparent," because this would be a nine-month relationship. Since Randy's grandpa had died recently, we knew it would be important for him to be with a "grandpa" who was able to take a genuine interest in him. Anna, our ever-cheerful classmate, helped out with a neighbor of hers who is blind, so she was the perfect match for an unresponsive resident who was also blind.

Connecting with the Elderly

We made biweekly visits to Rest Haven, with Kim planning one week and Dave and I planning the next. Our activities included pressing leaves, making tepees, singing, playing our instruments, doing word searches, frosting cookies, making wreaths, reading, and just enjoying one another's company (see Figure 8.2). For activities we met in the large dining room, but many residents invited the students to their rooms. Interestingly, our relationship with our "grandparents" provided a similar opportunity to talk about how we could best serve them. Although some were very talkative and generated fun (like the candy man who always had a trick or two followed by a treat), others hesitated to get involved in our projects or stayed on the sidelines when we gathered as a group. On some days Anna's "grandma" did not talk at all. We discussed our experiences with our own grandparents and the older people we knew in our neighborhoods and at church. We talked about their fears and the problems they face. Our questions led us to reading more about the elderly.

Strengthening Understanding through Reading

Kathryn McGuire was student teaching in our classroom during the fall semester, and she and I did a great deal of reflecting and dreaming together. She especially enjoyed our visits to Rest Haven and gave the students

FIGURE 8.2. Creston students invited Rest Haven residents to the school in June. Here Catherine Nicol enjoys ice cream with Jackson Buddingh and Seth Beals.

excellent advice on relating to their "grandparents." Kathryn also loved children's literature. She could often be found tucked away in a quiet spot reading a book a student had recommended to her. I loved listening in on her reading conferences with students because they were so interactive. Kathryn and I kept a journal together, usually writing in the evening as we thought back on the day. The journal became a springboard for after-school discussions comparing what we had read about learning to what we actually saw happening with our students. We shared our concerns about individual students, laughed over stories, and brainstormed to find an appropriate direction for literature-based reading with this particular group. It was out of this collaboration that Grandezvous was born. It was patterned after a six-week, districtwide reading program called Reading Rendezvous in which all our fourth- and fifth-graders read from a list of 30 books, respond in writing or drawing to each book, and conference with the teachers. Our students responded so well to this challenge that we decided to try it again with books about the elderly.

The two main components of Grandezvous were a large-group novel study and individualized reading from a recommended list of books. We divided the class into two heterogenous groups for a novel study using multiple copies of *That Wild Berries Should Grow* (Whelan, 1994) and *The War with Grandpa* (Smith, 1984). We chose these books because they portrayed a child's relationship with a grandparent. *That Wild Berries Should Grow* is about Elsa, a fifth-grader who lives in Detroit during the Great Depression. While recovering from an illness, she spends a summer on Lake Huron with her grandparents, where she learns to enjoy gardening, fishing, and exploring. Letters arrive from friends in Germany, telling Elsa's grandparents of their many troubles. Through shared experiences, Elsa gains a new understanding and appreciation for her grandparents. In *The War with Grandpa*, 10-year old Peter finds himself being moved upstairs to an attic bedroom when Grandpa must come to live with them. The war begins when Grandpa finds his belongings missing and an alarm clock going off in the middle of the night. Grandpa's understanding of Peter's feelings and his idea to build an apartment for himself in the basement help Peter learn that war is not an effective way to solve a problem.

Our emphasis in this component was on oral reading and discussion to help balance the silent reading we would do in the second component. This gave us a shared literature experience and an opportunity for Kathryn and me to help students develop their skills for expressive reading and observe their thinking processes.

Kathryn and I visited our librarian once again and gathered all the books we could on the elderly. We knew from the start that we wanted a balance of picture books and novels, both representing a wide range of reading difficulty. After two hours of sorting, we decided on our final list, feeling that it was very much in-process, even as we printed it out for the students (see Children's Books).

Our next step was to decide exactly what we expected of the students during this six-week period. Our expectations and awards were distributed at the start of Grandezvous to both students and parents:

Purpose: To strengthen bridges of understanding between generations
- Learn about problems older people face
- Appreciate ways older people enrich our lives
- Discover things to do with grandparents

Expectations
- Read a minimum of 500 pages
- Read one book in novel group
- Read two novels independently
- Read six picture books
- Prepare a reading response journal entry for each book, minimum six-line written response or a detailed drawing

Awards
- 250 pages—Book mark
- 500 pages—Pick a prize
- 750 pages—Pick a prize
- 1,000 pages—Order a free book

We felt Grandezvous was a great success. Parents reported increased reading at home, and we observed much informal book talk in the classroom, especially about the picture books. Eight students read over 1,000 pages, and everyone met the minimum requirements. Our book list experienced revision as students made suggestions for deletions and additions.

We also shared with parents our evaluation form reflecting our observations on the reading process (see Figure 8.3). At the conclusion of Grandezvous, students were given the opportunity to evaluate themselves on the reading process form. These were turned in to us along with the reading folder. Data for our evaluation on the form came from our anecdotal records during novel groups, entries in the reading response journal, notes from our conferences with individual students, self-evaluations, and informal observations.

Both to discover and to share with one another what had been learned about relating to the elderly, Kathryn and I went back to our objectives for Grandezvous to create an open-ended response where individual students could report what they had learned. After the forms were passed out, we encouraged groups to talk for about five minutes before writing.

FIGURE 8.3. Evaluation form for independent reading

GRANDEZVOUS EVALUATION

Reader_____

Evaluator_____

To the best of his/her ability, the reader:

	Grade	Comments
Seems to enjoy reading		
Reads silently for at least a half hour		
Comes prepared for a reading conference		
Can retell the story or information after reading		
Contributes thoughtful comments during reading conferences		
Completes written and artistic responses in sufficient detail		
Completes written and artistic responses neatly		
Keeps reading folder organized and up-to-date		
Meets deadlines		
Evaluates self and sets goals		

Grade Key:

    1 - Progressing Very Well
    2 - Progressing Satisfactorily
    3 - Experiencing Difficulty

Number of Pages Expected: _____

Number of Pages Read: _____

Final Grade: _____

Parents received both their child's response and the collated responses of the whole class (see Figure 8.4).

We had fun with Grandezvous, but more important, Kathryn and I felt we helped to build a stronger bridge between our students and their "grandparents" by heightening their awareness and understanding of another generation. We observed a more genuine compassion and appreciation for the elderly in the way many students related to their "grandparents" at Rest Haven, in their conversation in the classroom, and by the appearance of elderly characters in their writing during writing workshop.

EXPLORING STRUCTURAL BRIDGES

Each year in our classroom, all reading and writing time during February and March is devoted to researching a topic of choice, taking notes, writing a research paper, and teaching classmates what was learned. In January, I decided to go back to our bridge books and teach the basics of research by having the students write a short report using two sources, a bridge book and an encyclopedia. This would encourage comparison and integration of information. Since all "publishing" in fifth-grade is done on the computer, it was also an opportunity to add to their repertoire of computer skills. Topics chosen included the history of bridges, drawbridges, suspension bridges, care and safety, building materials, interesting facts, and the Golden Gate, Brooklyn, and Mackinac Bridges. Sarah wrote about history:

HISTORY OF BRIDGES

As we all know, bridges are useful in many ways. Most bridges we see are simple beam bridges made of concrete crossing a river.

Did you ever wonder what bridges looked like centuries ago? In prehistoric times man got across a body of water any way that they could, usually by a log fallen across a river or large stones leading to the other side.

Later people began to realize that they could make a bridge by themselves, by chopping a log over a river.

Soon they began to build more advanced bridges. One popular kind of bridge in prehistoric times in South America was the early suspension bridge. It looked a little like a hammock and it also swung like one.

Another design was thought up by the Persians in about 550 B.C. It was called a pontoon bridge. It used stuffed animal skins to float long boards. This was convenient in war time for the bridge was easily moved.

FIGURE 8.4. Composite of all student responses after reading about grandparents

LEARNING ABOUT GRANDPARENTS	Reader_____

List things you have learned from experience, your novel study book and the other books you have read so far in Grandezvous.

Problems older people face:

  LOSSES - hearing, hair, sight, memory, teeth, not able to do as many things independently
  HEALTH PROBLEMS - sickness, cancer, strokes, heart attacks, arthritis, bones break easily
  Death of a spouse
  Can't get around like they used to
  Difficult to stay in shape
  Depression

Ways older people enrich our lives:

  They teach us things, give us candy, are kind, tell stories, spoil us, encourage us, give wise advice, give us presents, love us, spend time with us, help us when we are in bad situations, tell us what it was like when they were young, and play games with us.

Things to do with grandparents:

  We can watch TV, have talks with them, play games, go to the movies or shopping, bake cookies, clean, make pictures, fly a kite, go on a vacation, help them, read with them, make them breakfast, decorate the Christmas tree, play pool, swim with them, crafts, make their bed, take a walk, watch the Rosebowl.

Conversation ideas:

  -the past   -how they are
  -if they liked school   -favorite video or TV show
  -what they like to do   -what they are reading
  -hobbies that we like   -people we know
  -jokes   -their children
  -what they did that week   -how old they are
  -what it would be like to live during a war

Around the middle ages draw bridges were used for castles. This was also convenient in war time.

Most bridges were made of wood or stone until the late 18th century when cast iron and wrought iron began to be used for such structures.

In the early 1800s in America covered bridges were used over small rivers and streams. These covered bridges were made of wood because it was cheap and there was allot of it. The only problem with the covered bridges was that they were not very strong and were easily taken out in floods.

Most large bridges you see now that are over bays or lakes are most likely suspension and made of concrete and steel.

Sarah Piersma, Grade 5. 1994

The information for this report was found in World Book Encyclopedia and *The bridge book* by Polly Carter.

Linking Fifth-Graders with an Engineering Company

Dave, the second-grade teacher, entered my room one morning and asked if I had seen the schedule for the West Michigan Science Festival. This was the first year for this community celebration of science, mathematics, and technology. Students were invited to participate in sectionals held at area businesses, manufacturers, and educational organizations. They were offering a sectional on bridges! Here was our opportunity to talk to an engineer. We took a bus to Fishbeck, Thompson, Carr & Huber, Inc. (FTC&H), a consulting engineering, scientific, and architectural firm, where we were shown slides of local bridges, a video of famous bridge collapses, and how bridges are designed on the computer. We also learned about the different materials used in building bridges and the strength of the triangle in the bridge structure. The students asked many questions about the cost of bridges, safety, how long it took to plan and build a bridge, and what school subjects were important if one wanted to become an engineer.

Observing Structural Bridges

A natural follow-up to our FTC&H experience was to visit some local bridges. I chose to go to the small park by the Ada covered bridge because there are three bridges over the Thornapple River on that site. The covered bridge is used only by walkers and bikers and is a beautiful historical landmark. On one side of the covered bridge is a railroad bridge and on the other is a highway girder bridge. I prepared a questionnaire, including safety rules (see Figure 8.5), and gave each student a clipboard with sheets of draw-

FIGURE 8.5. Eric's bridge questionnaire

Eric

VISIT TO THE ADA COVERED BRIDGE

Important Rules:

1. Stay as a group with the person with whom you rode.
2. The river is dangerous, stay back.
3. Place all lunch litter in our trash bag.
4. Gather as a group when you hear the whistle.

Your assignment:

* This is a field trip, not a picnic! You are here to learn, observe and create.
* Answer as many of the following questions that you can.
* Find a quiet spot and decide whether you will draw the bridge or write a poem about it.

1. About when was the bridge built and for what purpose?

   1857

2. Look closely at the inside structure. Draw the plan for support trusses.

   [drawing of support trusses]

3. Look underneath the bridge. How is the roadway supported? (Show in a drawing if you like.)

   2 long wooden beam supports and the foundation is two concrete walls.

4. There are three bridges at this sight: the covered bridge, the railroad bridge, and the automobile bridge. How can you compare them?

   They all have concrete foundations, one is made of wood, one is made of steel, and the other is made of concrete and steel. All three go over the same river.

5. Describe any evidence of bridge deterioration we learned about at Fishbeck?

   Wood is rotting a little, looks wet and a lot of nails are sticking out, The concrete is cracked in a lot of places.

ing and writing paper to take along. We divided into groups of four, with mothers heading each group. By listening to their conversation about the bridges, I became aware of how much we had learned. While we were there, a long train passed over the railroad bridge and a man came to test the quality of the river water. Figure 8.6 shows Seth's poem and drawing of the covered bridge.

Building Toothpick Bridges

I looked forward to revisiting the toothpick bridge project both because of its success the previous year and because I was anxious to see what effect our study would have on the quality of the bridges the students built. After dividing the students into heterogeneous groups of four, we rearranged the room so that each group was clustered around a table which would be the company headquarters. We distributed copies of the blacklines provided in the book, reviewed the history of bridge development, and looked again at the basic bridge types. Each company was given an account of $1,550,000.00, checks, balance sheets, and order forms. Their first challenge would be to decide who would be responsible for the jobs of project director, architect, carpenter, transportation chief, and accountant. Pollard (1985) defines the job duties very clearly, and few questions were asked. I ran the warehouse from which they would need to purchase land, lumber (toothpicks), welding material (glue), and building-plans paper. One of the project director's jobs was to keep a daily journal of the company's progress, recording any problems and their solutions. Notice the problems faced by Hangerockhouse Bridges and Engineering Company in Katie's entries on days 3 and 4.

Day 3
The night before Anna took home the plans to work on them. Her dad who does blue prints for a living, and studied it for college, told her that ours would take too long and not hold anything, so today we changed all our plans. Josh made the squares on land for supports. Our architect finished all the buiding plan also, we started building our foundation.

Day 4
We made the supports to crooked so we took them apart to start over, but then we decided to make all our toothpicks double to make it stronger. News flash—Anna just told me we don't have enough money to make them doubles. Now we are putting a toothpick through the middle of the cube but Ben was experiment-

FIGURE 8.6. Seth Beal's poem and drawing of the Ada covered bridge

the Silent water flowing bye, very big clouds filling the sky, the hiding birds shout thier cry, I'm so hungry I want I'll die think

Seth

ing with tooth picks and we decided to make triangles in our cube, this I think will work the best of all the ideas we have had. (From Katie's journal, 1994)

One specification was that the final structure had to match the blueprint. The architect kept the plans out during the building process and referred to them often when advising the carpenter. Figure 8.7 shows Laura working from the blueprint to build the bridge.

The five companies designed their bridges very differently; yet when bridge-breaking day came, all of them surprised us by the weight they could support. We ran a pencil through the sides of each bridge, across the road-bed, and suspended a 32 ounce plastic cup by string from the pencil. Weight was slowly added to the cup, first 100 grams, then 50, until we reached 2,000. The weakest bridge began to break at about 2,100 grams. The strongest held over 2,500 grams. When we lifted the plastic cup ourselves, we were amazed that toothpicks and glue could support that much weight. Most of the groups "surrendered" when the bridge began to sink, quickly removing the weight and repairing the damage. One group enjoyed watching the total destruction of their bridge.

FIGURE 8.7. Laura carefully adds glue to strengthen the bridge

The building project provided a wonderful opportunity to integrate and apply all we had learned about bridges from books, videos, an engineer, and our observation of real bridges. As the students chose pieces from the bridge folders to be placed in their portfolios, Brad wrote this reflection:

> It's been a real experience building bridges. I was the architect for our company. I've learned a lot about planning and how to deal with problems when they happen. We were the first company to begin construction. The part I liked best was telling the carpenter how to build the bridge. I thought it would be hard but it was actually kind of cool. The only bad part was that I couldn't actually help build the bridge. Overall it's been really fun and I've enjoyed myself.

REFLECTING ON OUR CONNECTING

One of the most effective tools for understanding one another, evaluating learning, and planning direction is the journal. It was through the reading response journal that I could communicate with and learn about each student as we read about bridges and grandparents. My own journal reminds me of where I have been in my thinking and is a place to record my dreams for where I am headed as a learner and teacher.

The students' journals, the joint student teacher/teacher journal, and my own journal all help me keep my finger on the pulse of my classroom. They help me tap into the gifts and wonderings of my fellow learners, standing as an essential part of collaboration.

I view my classroom as a community of learners and the greater community as a classroom. Connecting to the world outside the school enhances and gives purpose for learning inside the school. Our learning with the second-graders, the residents at Rest Haven, the engineer at FTC&H, and at the local bridges built bridges from school to the real world. We have a responsibility as teachers to watch for opportunities for ourselves and our students to learn from and to serve our community.

This year's journey with bridges included so much more than I have chronicled here. In October we received a plea for help from a fellow teacher who had decided to spend a year teaching in Haiti. Our students and teachers helped set up a reading program comprised of their favorite books, gathered the money to purchase the books, and sent them off along with a box full of incentives and many prayers. We learned so much about life in a Third-World country through that bridge to Haiti that spanned the year and found ourselves listening very closely to the news about the political unrest they were experiencing.

I am anxious to continue with Bridges next year and see what will happen with a new group of learners. I think it would be fun to include the second-graders in the picture book component of Grandezvous and to have the second- and fifth-graders write and "publish" growing-up stories with the Rest Haven residents.

Bridges—a journey that began with a plan, but one that welcomed the surprises along the way. None of us in Room 307 will ever look at a bridge the same way. We will be more aware of the structure itself and probably want to see the underside! The sight of a bridge will trigger memories of our year of learning together and many satisfying friendships with peers and "grandparents."

REFERENCES

Cianciolo, Patricia J. (1990). *Picture books for children*. Chicago: American Library Association.

Kobrin, Beverly (1988). *Eyeopeners! How to choose and use children's books about real people, places, and things*. New York: Penguin.

Pollard, Jeanne (1985). *Building toothpick bridges*. Palo Alto, CA: Dale Seymour Publications.

Tchudi, Stephen (1991). *Travels across the curriculum: Models for interdisciplinary learning*. New York: Scholastic.

CHILDREN'S BOOKS

Nonfiction Books About Bridges

Ardley, Neil. (1990). *How we build bridges*. Ada, OK: Garrett Educational Corporation.

Carter, Polly. (1992). *The bridge book*. New York: Simon & Schuster.

Cooper, Jason. (1991). *Bridges: Man-made wonders*. Vero Beach, FL: Rourke.

Gringhuis, Dirk. (1959). *Big Mac: The building of the world's biggest bridge*. New York: Macmillan.

Pelta, Kathy. (1987). *Bridging the Golden Gate*. Minneapolis: Lerner.

Robbins, Ken. (1991). *Bridges*. New York: Dial.

Royston, Angela. (1991). *Buildings, bridges, and tunnels*. New York: Warwick.

Sandak, Cass R. (1983). *Bridges*. New York: Franklin Watts.

Spangenburg, Ray, & Moser, Diane K. (1991). *The story of America's bridges*. New York: Facts on File.

St. George, Judith. (1982). *The Brooklyn Bridge: They said it couldn't be built*. New York: Putnam.

Wilson, Hugh. (Ed.). (1991). *Structures*. Alexandria, VA: Time-Life Books.

Novels About Grandparents

Ames, Mildred. (1990). *Grandpa Jake and the grand Christmas*. New York: Scribner.
Blakeslee, Ann R. (1989). *After the fortune cookies*. New York: Putnam.
Brancato, Robin F. (1982). *Sweet bells jangled out of tune*. New York: Knopf.
Byars, Betsy. (1987). *A blossom promise*. New York: Delacorte.
Clifford, Eth. (1985). *The remembering box*. New York: Beech Tree Books.
Fakih, Kimberly Olson. (1994). *High on the hog*. New York: Farrar, Straus & Giroux.
Fox, Paula. (1993). *Western wind*. New York: Orchard.
Grimoto, Jean Davies. (1990). *Take a chance Gramps!* New York: Joy Street/Little,
    Brown.
Hartling, Peter. (1990). *Old John*. New York: Morrow.
Haseley, Dennis. (1991). *Shadows*. New York: Farrar, Straus & Giroux.
Hobbs, Will. (1989). *Bearstone*. New York: Atheneum.
Holl, Kristi D. (1985). *The rose beyond the wall*. New York: Atheneum.
Larrabee, Lisa. (1993). *Grandmother Five Baskets*. Illustrated by Lori Sawyer. Tuc-
    son: Harbinger House.
MacLachlan, Patricia. (1991). *Journey*. New York: Dell.
Maggio, Rasalie. (1990). *The music box Christmas*. New York: Morrow.
Nixon, Joan Lowery. (1983). *The gift*. New York: Macmillan.
Nixon, Joan Lowery. (1985). *Maggie, too*. San Diego: Harcourt Brace Jovanovich.
Rylant, Cynthia. (1992). *Missing May*. New York: Orchard.
Slote, Alfred. (1990). *The trading game*. Philadelphia: Lippincott.
Smith, Robert Kimmel. (1984). *The war with Grandpa*. New York: Delacorte.
Whelan, Gloria. (1994). *That wild berries should grow*. Grand Rapids, MI: Eerdmans.
Wright, Betty Ren. (1981). *Getting rid of Marjorie*. New York: Holiday House.

Picture Books About Grandparents

Ackerman, Karen. (1988). *Song and dance man*. Illustrated by Stephen Gammell.
    New York: Knopf.
Ackerman, Karen. (1990). *Just like Max*. Illustrated by George Schmidt. New York:
    Knopf.
Aliki. (1979). *The two of them*. New York: Greenwillow.
Bahr, Mary. (1992). *The memory box*. Illustrated by David Cunningham. Morton
    Grove, IL: Albert Whitman.
Blegvad, Lenore. (1993). *Once upon a time and Grandma*. Illustrated by Erik Blegvad.
    New York: Margaret K. Elderry Books.
Bunting, Eve. (1989). *The Wednesday surprise*. Illustrated by Beth Peck. New York:
    Clarion/Houghton.
Bunting, Eve. (1994). *Sunshine home*. Illustrated by Diane DeGroat. New York:
    Clarion.
Carlstrom, Nancy White. (1990). *Grandpappy*. Illustrated by Laurel Molk. Boston:
    Little, Brown.
Daly, Niki. (1986). *Not so fast Songololo*. New York: Atheneum.

dePaola, Tomie. (1981). *Now one foot, now the other*. New York: Putnam.

Egger, Bettina. (1987). *Marianne's grandmother*. Illustrated by Sita Jucker. New York: Dutton.

Flournoy, Valerie. (1985). *The patchwork quilt*. Illustrated by Jerry Pinkney. New York: Dial.

Fox, Mem. (1985). *Wilfrid Gordon McDonald Partridge*. Illustrated by Julie Vivas. New York: Kane/Miller.

Fox, Mem. (1989). *Shoes from Grandpa*. Illustrated by Patricia Mullins. New York: Orchard.

Goble, Paul. (1989). *Beyond the ridge*. New York: Bradbury.

Greenfield, Eloise. (1980). *Grandmama's joy*. Illustrated by Carol Byard. New York: Philomel.

Griffith, Helen V. (1986). *Georgia music*. Illustrated by James Stevenson. New York: Greenwillow.

Griffith, Helen V. (1994). *Dream meadow*. Illustrated by Nancy Barnet. New York: Greenwillow.

Hall, Donald. (1994). *The farm summer 1942*. Illustrated by Barry Moser. New York: Dial.

Haskins, Francine. (1993). *Things I like about Grandma*. Chicago: Children's Press.

Johnston, Tony. (1991). *Grandpa's song*. Illustrated by Brad Sneed. New York: Dial.

Lasky, Kathryn. (1988). *Sea swan*. Illustrated by Catherine Stock. New York: Macmillan.

Levinson, Riki. (1985). *Watch the stars come out*. Illustrated by Diane Goode. New York: Dutton.

Mathis, Sharon Bell. (1975). *The hundred penny box*. Illustrated by Leo and Diane Dillon. New York: Viking.

Moore, Elaine. (1994). *Deep river*. Illustrated by Henri Sorensen. New York: Simon & Schuster.

Moore, Elaine. (1994). *Grandma's garden*. Illustrated by Dan Andreasen. New York: Lothrop, Lee & Shepard.

Palacco, Patricia. (1992). *Mrs. Katz and Tush*. New York: Dell.

Sakai, Kimiko. (1990). *Sachiko means happiness*. Illustrated by Tomie Arai. Chicago: Children's Press.

Schwartz, David M. (1991). *Supergrandpa*. Illustrated by Bert Dodson. New York: Lothrop, Lee & Shepard.

Tan, Amy. (1992). *The moon lady*. Illustrated by Gretchen Schields. New York: Macmillan.

Upham, Elizabeth. (1985). *Grandmother's locket*. Illustrated by Maureen O'Keefe Hall. Monroe, MI: Monroe County Library System.

Yolen, Jane. (1977). *The seeing stick*. Illustrated by Remy Charlip & Demestra Maraslis. New York: Crowell.

Yolen, Jane. (1993). *Honkers*. Illustrated by Leslie Baker. Boston: Little, Brown.

Yolen, Jane. (1994). *Grandad Bill's song*. Illustrated by Melissa Bay Mathis. New York: Philomel.

Autobiographical Photoessays About Grandparents

Farber, Norma. (1979). *How does it feel to be old?* New York: Puffin.
Greenfield, Eloise. (1979). *Childtimes: A three-generation memoir*. New York: Crowell.
Khalsa, Dayal Daur. (1986). *Tales of a gambling grandma*. New York: Clarkson Potter.
LeShan, Eda. (1984). *Grandparents: A special kind of love*. New York: Macmillan.
Vineberg, Ethel. (1987). *Grandmother came from Dworitz*. Plattsburgh, NY: Tundra.

CHAPTER 9

A Sense of Balance

A First-Grade Literary Community

Janice V. Kristo and Mary H. Giard

It is fitting that the success stories in this book begin and end with first-graders. Chapter 2 describes a beginning venture into a shared curriculum. This final chapter presents a classroom totally immersed in integrating all aspects of the children's learning. We hope this last chapter will answer any remaining questions about the role of children's literature in making these connections.

When teachers make the transition from a traditional classroom in which each subject is taught separately to integrating reading, writing, spelling, and the content areas, it can be a leap into the unknown. There is a danger of jumping on the bandwagon of integration by filling the room with materials and not offering the leadership and direct teaching that the children need to focus their learning. As a result, many questions arise and discouragement sets in, especially if professional collaborations have not been established.

In this chapter, a veteran teacher answers important questions about planning and management presented by a frequent visitor to her classroom. Janice Kristo, University of Maine professor, entered Mary Giard's classroom in Bangor, Maine, six years ago when she overheard a riveting discussion about books. To her amazement, these were first-graders conversing with their teacher, not fifth- or sixth-graders as she expected. This began a two-year commitment of observing Mary in action. Watching and listening to Mary Giard, videotaping the class, and keeping copious notes helped Jan Kristo to understand how vital it is for a teacher to love books, know her students well, and know how to make the connections between the children and the books. From this collaboration, Jan finds that she listens to her own college students more carefully and helps them to reflect about books in deeper and more meaningful ways. Mary Giard notes that Jan's constant questioning of her beliefs and practices causes her to think more deeply about her teaching.

Mary Giard has established a balance in her classroom between teacher direction and the children's instigation of classroom learning. This balance generates a positive environment in which she can see the children growing daily. The environment is constructed thoughtfully and carefully.

This chapter begins with a dialogue between Jan and Mary about Mary's beliefs about using literature and her planning procedures for inviting powerful conversations connecting literature across the curriculum. They then go on to discuss key points about the successful use of literature throughout the curriculum in this classroom.

A DIALOGUE ABOUT LITERATURE
ACROSS THE CURRICULUM

JAN: Mary, what are your beliefs about using literature in your first-grade classroom?

MARY: I believe that good literature is the cornerstone of learning for a number of reasons. When I think about where we live, a somewhat isolated Maine city, I realize how essential it is for children to have access to their experiences, other cultures, other ways of life, different people, and the arts. Literature can help children transport themselves, through their imagination, to other places and times. Books are vehicles to help them make connections they might not necessarily make on their own and to live lives they might never have otherwise. Literature provides a common experience for every child in the classroom. We all have something to talk about as a result of books we read and I share aloud—no one gets left out. In the process, we build a literary community. Consequently, these experiences make children's trips to the library or bookstore a highly charged experience because they recognize familiar books, authors, and subjects. That is a powerful discovery for young minds that, I believe, helps them to make more informed choices about books they read.

JAN: Let's talk about your approach of using literature throughout the curriculum.

MARY: One thing that I have really thought about is trying to make sure that the books I choose are age- and content-appropriate, and that I am not just making haphazard selections. I think sometimes teachers feel everything has to fit the theme or topic, and that they become ruled by the material rather than really thinking about what children need to know and what they would like to learn. That is, I don't approach a topic by find-

ing a collection of books and trying to make them fit. When I start thinking about what I am going to do, I figure out what will be good basic information with which to start. I try to find books that will reinforce and/
or extend our areas of study.

JAN: When I talk with teachers, they are always amazed at teachers
like you who seem able to pull together a collection of books from a wide
variety of genres that complement an area of study. What is your process
of finding what books you will use?

MARY: My book collection did not develop overnight. For many years
I have browsed libraries and bookstores. Consequently, I spend a lot of
my own money on books. This has made me more selective about what I
buy, so that I do not end up with a bunch of fluff. I read *Horn Book* and
think about what I buy before I buy it so that I purchase high-quality books.
Scanning new children's literature textbooks also is a quick way to access
a large body of information. Another source, for me, is talking with people
like you who read the new books. I would recommend that teachers make
frequent visits to bookstores and museum shops for books. For instance,
in our area, the Hudson Museum at the University of Maine has a great
selection of Native American books and artifacts. When I travel, I try to
buy books that I cannot find here. Since I have taught first grade for a while,
I have a good sense of what children typically enjoy at this age. Increas-
ingly, I have found that girls and boys enjoy nonfiction, so I have really
beefed up my nonfiction collection over the past few years. They also love
science, so I purchase lots of science-related books.

JAN: When you are planning a unit, how much of it are you organizing ahead or does it emerge in another way? Many teachers focus first on
writing goals, objectives, and activities before actually working with students. Is this how you do it?

MARY: No, I don't. First of all, I do not buy any packaged thematic units.
I want to know that what we are doing is as authentic as possible and meets
our needs. I do not need a publisher to give me a lot of cute things to do.
Very often, I find that published units are very formulaic, with little intel-
lectual depth. I look at what the curricular issues are for us. Integrating
the curriculum has become a bandwagon that both teachers and publishers are riding for all it's worth. Teachers often seem to feel that *everything*
within their day must be linked to the topic of study in order for them to
be considered good teachers who provide meaningful experiences for their
children. Many teachers scan catalogues searching for activities to go along
with books or themes they plan to study. I don't do that. My students are
different each year, and so I do not assume that my topics of study will be
the same, nor do I think the materials I use with one group will automati-
cally be effective and meaningful with another.

Although our school system does have a curriculum, we are given the freedom to meet the goals in our own ways, using our judgment about how to deal with issues. I have a great deal of freedom to pursue and explore aspects of the curriculum that children find most meaningful and engaging. With this in mind, one of the things that I do early on in the year is to discuss at length with children what topics they want to investigate. I web this information as they talk; this serves as a springboard for me to find out what they want to learn. I look for commonalties among topics. This webbing process broadens their horizons because they get to look at other children's interests. There may be topics they have never considered before. What I find is that as the year unfolds, we weave a lot of their own ideas into what we are doing. Other things emerge that sometimes take precedence, but I think the important issue is that I start the year with the expectation that children will contribute and be part of the decision-making process. Oftentimes, they will pick things that sound interesting to them but that they do not know much about. I need to think about connections to broader topics so we are not just answering a specific question. For instance, we have studied Van Gogh and this coming week, Monet. Concurrently, we are studying Impressionism and Post-Impressionism. Now the children want to learn about other artists and styles of art. I also try not to give them answers. I orchestrate learning so that they can discover things themselves. As the year progresses, we may pick a topic during which they become the primary researchers and make their own connections. Each time we study a major topic, we think of different ways to "publicize" what we learn so that we can share it with our families and the community. For example, when we studied the Mayan civilization earlier this year, we produced a video in which we talked about the many things we had discovered about this vanished civilization.

In any event, every time we begin a new area of study the first thing we do is a web to discover what they already know, and we plan from there. In some instances I choose the topic, and other times they choose what we study.

JAN: Talk about how you assess what students do in their unit work.

MARY: I am relatively informal when it comes to this sort of thing. Within our school system, there is not anything specific about assessment in science, social studies, and the arts, in particular. What I tend to do is pose a question and have the children do something with it. As an example, when we studied the Mayans the assessment was the video they produced. I also listen carefully to how they talk about what they learned. This helps me to shape subsequent things that we do.

JAN: What are students' reactions to literature in general and working with literature throughout the curriculum?

MARY: First of all, I don't think that the children notice that literature is woven throughout the curriculum. It's such a natural aspect of my planning that it should not seem unusual to them. However, I do think that they appreciate the ways in which literature can amplify their understandings of particular topics.

JAN: How do parents react to your use of literature throughout the curriculum?

MARY: Parents begin to understand that learning and discovery do not begin and end at the classroom door. They realize that there are countless numbers of outstanding books for children on almost any topic you choose. This is very liberating for many parents, because it allows them to guide and participate in their children's learning. In addition, these books are of such high quality that many parents make new discoveries themselves. It extends the model of lifelong learning from the classroom to the home.

JAN: Mary, you've used literature for many years now. Has your thinking changed in any way in terms of using literature in the classroom?

MARY: Yes, I've always been interested in having literature as the centerpiece of my classroom. The thing that has changed for me is that I've refined how I use it. I have become much more critical in my selection of materials. Now, I think much more about how books will connect with each other and how I can make each experience both meaningful and engaging for children. Everything I choose is intended to help them continue with their learning. Books are such an investment that I need to spend more time with my selections rather than rushing through them. I focus on quality rather than quantity. What is important to me is that we come to some understanding of a text beyond the literal level. I want to know why we read a particular book. What did we learn from exploring and responding to a book? I like to experiment with the notion of digging deeper into a book, taking time with it and being relaxed enough to see what emerges from both me and the children. Good books can't be rushed; they need to be savored. In that way, challenging books become more accessible to all of my students.

In the past I was guilty of what I call the "book flood model." Children spent too much time on their own trying to read texts that were too difficult. I did not provide them enough support to tackle the materials. For example, I have always used the *The Legend of the Bluebonnet* (dePaola, 1983) when studying Native Americans. As I think about that particular book now, there are so many concepts and literary conventions that are new to children that I would share it aloud and discuss the historical and cultural issues to make it more meaningful and accessible to the children.

JAN: Do you ever have concerns about the utilitarian use of books? I always remember Charlotte Huck saying once that we forget that books are for pleasure and enjoyment and rather we look at them as things to use.

MARY: Time is precious in my day. If possible I try to have a purpose for a book that goes beyond just pleasure. What's essential is my approach to and delivery of a book. When I read aloud, it is a community-building event; it is a restorative act. However, even though it's a calm and reflective time, there is always a purpose underlying the book selection. Sometimes, it may just be for pleasure. Still, I try to be economical, so as often as possible I mix pleasure with purpose.

JAN: As I look around your room, I notice a lot of the books are challenging—picture books and chapter books that teachers ordinarily would use with older students. You share sophisticated books with your first-graders, and they seem very capable of understanding them. How do you structure your read-aloud to achieve this?

MARY: When I introduce a book, I talk about it a lot before reading it to the children. In addition, I often bring an object or artifact related to the book to show the children, particularly if the ideas or concepts are not familiar to them. One of the other things I try to do is to poll the group and find out who knows what before I start. Some child in class may have experience or expertise in the area we are investigating. If possible, I do not want to be the only one imparting knowledge. Therefore, I do not make assumptions. As I read aloud, we do a lot of talking throughout the book. I do not wait until the end of the book to invite interaction. I ask children what they think.

JAN: Your read-aloud times seem so relaxed. You do it in such a way that I really have never seen a teacher do before. Obviously, primary teachers read aloud to kids, but the message might be, "This is a good book, kids, and I'm doing a great job reading it aloud, and then we'll talk about it later." You maintain a lot of eye contact with children. You use your hands a lot to elaborate on ideas, and you invite interaction. There is a sense of patience in terms of reading through a book so that you can, at times, stop and explain something or ask children what they are thinking. In other words, that doesn't bother or annoy you like it would some teachers whose primary purpose is to get through a book and for students to save all their remarks or comments. It is an annoyance to some teachers to have so much conversing going on throughout a read-aloud. I see that during your read-alouds there is time for dialogue rather than it being just a time for you to read aloud a book.

MARY: I think that it makes the read-aloud much more engrossing for children, because that is when connections are made. It has got to be an active time. I don't want them to be passive. I want them to be fully engaged in the read-aloud. I see it as an opportunity to tap metacognitive activity. We take time to talk about what they think, what they understand, what they know, what they bring to the book, and what they take from it.

JAN: Teachers go about creating different kinds of opportunities for children to explore literature across the curriculum. They all have their own success stories to share. What is your success story?

MARY: I can't think of a specific success story, but as I think about what I have done over the years, I look at what has been successful. What are things that have worked well? I have been successful with refining my questioning techniques. Good questioning is essential. It is the driving force for all learning in my classroom. I try always to get the children to ask, "Why?" Why are they making the choices they are making? It is like being 2 years old again, when asking, "Why? Why? Why?" is so important. I want children to do that so that we get to the bottom of how we make decisions. I want them to be able to articulate and substantiate what it is they are talking about. For me, it's imperative to keep asking them questions: "How do you know that?" "How did you figure that out?" "Tell me more about that." "Explain what you mean." I want to get at the roots of how and why they think the way that they do not only to help me facilitate their learning, but also to help them arrive at deeper levels of self-knowledge. That to me is the greatest success story.

Studying Native Americans

JAN: Would you talk about the Native American unit? How did you go about choosing that topic and planning your unit?

MARY: This year all four first-grade teachers worked together to design a social studies unit. One of the areas in our curriculum is families and communities. We decided that each class would investigate different cultures in the United States: Native Americans (which our class studied), Asian Americans, African Americans, and Latinos. I thought about whether our focus would be on Native Americans from Maine or from other areas in the United States. In the end, I decided to investigate several Native American cultures so that children would have an opportunity to broaden their knowledge of Native Americans across the United States. We used the map to locate Native Americans from the Northwest, the Southwest, the Southeast, the Woodlands, and the Plains. I used literature to introduce each culture. Interestingly, children soon began to bring in all kinds of things related to Native Americans. The class next to ours became very curious about all of the projects we were doing, and they started to bring things in for us to look at, too. So, the unit expanded from there and ended up being a broader and deeper study than I had anticipated.

When I talked to the children at the beginning of the unit, I discovered they knew very little about Native Americans and, in many cases, had stereotypical views of them. I was actually surprised at the responses. Although the children live in an isolated community, they, on the whole, seemed accepting of people. I was concerned about the difference in perspectives between boys and girls. Many of the girls tended to act fearful, while the boys were interested in the more warlike behavior glorified by popular culture. After polling the group to assess their background knowledge, I suggested that we had a lot to learn before we could make judgments about another culture. Therefore we needed to develop a plan of action. I knew, then, that it was important to find nonstereotypical literature about Native Americans (see Bibliography of Native American Literature at the end of the chapter).

That discussion led to part two of our planning for the unit. We brainstormed a web of questions we wanted to answer in order to become more knowledgeable about Native Americans. The children generated these questions and issues: Who are Native Americans? Where do they live? What do they eat? What do they wear? How large are their families? What do their houses look like? Do they have special traditions— music? art? stories? What are differences in their languages? What is important to them? How do they make decisions and rules?

These questions established a framework from which to start our investigations. By preparing questions at the end of our school week (Friday), we all had the weekend to gather materials and question people around us about their understandings, knowledge, and opinions. The children had not expressed a preference for any particular part of the country, so I made the decision to start with the Southwest for a number of reasons. First of all, I have a strong affinity for southwestern indigenous cultures. I have traveled extensively in the Southwest and investigated the native cultures in that area. However, my interests extend beyond the Southwest to indigenous cultures throughout the United States. In my travels I have collected numerous books, artifacts, and materials not only to expand my knowledge but also to provide vicarious experiences for my students. Consequently, I have a well-rounded selection of books and materials that I have gathered over the years. I dug out all my books that weekend and browsed through them to organize a plan to get our class started on Monday. I decided to sort them by geographic area so that if, for example, we read about southwestern people, we focused on them for an extended period of time to become immersed in their cultures.

Monday morning came and some of the children brought items from home: books, moccasins, a small totem pole, leather goods, and postcards from the Southwest. We set up a table in a corner of our room with a book display and added the items that the children brought to a large table. On the floor were three baskets filled with Native American books. These materials stayed in that location throughout the unit, so all of us could browse and have access to the information whenever we needed it. That afternoon we looked at the web we had developed the previous Friday and reviewed our questions. We took some time to share what the children had brought. I also gave short book talks to share the variety of literature available to them.

Often I see teachers make a beautiful display of books and materials in their rooms. They have invested so much time making it attractive that they are reluctant to let children freely explore the display because their display soon looks like just a pile of books. Thus the children who need to immerse themselves in these materials are excluded from exploring them. I believe it is essential that children have free access to as many resources as possible.

Once we had all shared, I began our unit by reading *The Legend of the Bluebonnet* (dePaola, 1983). This book is by definition fiction, but what *is* it? Realistic fiction? Myth? This one story initiated a deep and focused exploration of fact versus fiction. Each day we delved into another book. By reading aloud, we began to create a common foundation of knowledge from which to build. While the readings seemed to fascinate the children, they did not fully answer their questions about Native Americans, and, so, other questions began to arise. The children began to compare and contrast the homes, names, dress, hardships, and characters across cultures. Questions of what is fact and what is fiction emerged.

We also explored storytelling from the Southwest. When we discussed the Pueblo cultures, I brought in my collection of Storytellers (clay figures depicting the oral tradition of the culture). We talked about them, and the children sketched their own Storyteller. After reading examples of Navajo and Hopi tales, children wrote their own tales and designed a clay Storyteller to go with it. From this we produced a Storyteller book and made copies for everyone. We balanced absolutely free topic choice for writing with more directed writing experiences to correspond with our study of Native Americans.

What began to happen next—and I find this occurs often—is that children chose to focus their writing on topics we had discussed about Native Americans. They wrote their own versions of Native American tales, such as this one by David.

The Indian Warriors went back to their teepees. It was nighttime, with no stars or moon. It was an empty sky. The warriors slept. One warrior was not able to sleep so he decided to hunt buffalo. He looked and looked but could not find one.

Finally, the warrior found a buffalo. He turned his head. Then he turned back toward the buffalo. The buffalo had disappeared! The warrior continued his hunt. Seeing the buffalo was a sign. He knew he would find buffaloes for his people.

David, age 6

It was David's turn to share his writing with the class. He brought his warrior draft to the writing sharing circle to receive input from us. He told us he got his idea from the many stories we had read. He had made the choice to write about the warrior in his draft book; it had not been an assignment given to the entire class. I sat back in the circle listening to him share and watching the other members of the class ask their questions and make comments:

I liked the way you used language that sounds like the Native Americans. You made your piece sound authentic. How did you do that?
I liked the way you combined a lot of what we have learned, but you didn't copy any of the authors or tales. You made it your own. What will you add next?
You made your idea sound so beautiful. It didn't sound like the kind of story we thought Native American pieces were a few weeks ago. It sounded like a real Native American piece.

JAN: Mary, in what way would you summarize what happened as a result of this unit of study?
MARY: Our unit evolved into quite an investigation. The more we read, learned, and heard, the more our views changed, and the more we wanted to learn. We planned on a month for our unit and spent about an hour a day learning about Native American cultures. Our allotted time went by quickly, and we had not clearly exhausted our investigation. Although it no longer remained our major focus, we periodically brought in new materials and artifacts. Children continued to write about native cultures, and I noticed a transference of what they had learned into new experiences. They began to broaden their understandings of different cultures. We came up with more ways to share what we had learned. During the final week of our unit, all of the first-grades gathered for a cultural festival. We shared food and artifacts from the respective cultures we studied. In addition, we had a week of sharing cultural crafts. The classes rotated each day, so all first grades experienced designing a Native American craft in my class. My children, in turn, designed Latino, African American, and Asian American crafts. Each afternoon culminated in viewing a filmstrip,

having a book read aloud, or examining cultural artifacts. Finally, each child worked on an object to take home and share with family members. Several children, like Anna, chose to make a Hopi Kachina doll, while David designed a Zuni hand mask used in a Native American dance (see Figure 9.1). We focused on what emerged naturally from the children's questions and our readings. Students set the learning agenda.

We certainly had learned a lot in a month. Stereotypes fell by the wayside. It became apparent that all cultures have very strong and meaningful traditions. By reading fiction and nonfiction we were able to piece information together. We realized that we could also survey other people, go to museums, watch films, and look at magazines. Our unit of study not only taught us about a subject of interest to us, it taught us how to learn about it together. It taught us how to observe and to question, and by questioning we came to understand that not all we hear or read is true. Certainly we had learned about other cultures, but in the end we had learned so much more than that. As far as I was concerned, our mission had been accomplished. We had learned some things, and we realized how much we had to reevaluate our preconceptions. The children, once again, learned that knowledge and discovery are multilayered, and we had merely peeled away one layer; we had whetted our appetites to learn more.

ACCOUNTING FOR SUCCESS

What accounts for a teacher's success? This is an easy question to pose, but a difficult one to answer with pat responses. Newkirk (1992) says it well when he describes what occurs in Pat McLure's combined first/second grade classroom. He states, "Even for those of us who spend time in her classroom, Pat's style is elusive, difficult to articulate as a set of principles" (p. 116). Newkirk refers to this challenge as "the enigma of instinct." Similar to Pat, Mary bases many of her decisions upon all that she has read, but more important, she knows her children and literature so well that one has to spend time watching and listening to the interactions that occur about books to begin to appreciate her success as a teacher.

What one observes in Mary's classroom leaves longlasting impressions about the relationship she has with her children. A day spent in Mary's classroom seems to float from one seamless conversation to another. *Conversation* seems to be the best word to describe the interchanges Mary has with her students. These conversations are rippled with rich inquiring moments. Mary always wants to know more about how her students are thinking, how they are reacting to books, and to everything, for that matter. Action is the name of the game in this classroom! In one sense Mary's

FIGURE 9.1. Studying Native Americans. Left: Anna proudly displays her Kachina doll. Right: David models his Zuni hand mask.

"teaching mode" is no different from the way she is with students before school, after school, or when she sees them at the mall. Mary's "signature teaching style" is marked by an inquisitiveness to learn, a genuine interest in what children think, her own puzzlements about the world, and her joie de vivre! So, how does one go about accurately describing a teacher such as this? From our years together reflecting on practice and talking about what matters in teaching, we offer the following points as central to creating memorable moments with books, the very important ingredient in this literary community.

Instigating Reading

Mary loves literature; it is her avocation and her life. With over 12 years of teaching she has refined her tastes in books, explored many ways to find out about books, and reflected on her use of literature with first-graders. Mary is never quite content with maintaining the status quo in terms of her use of literature. Since it is the very backbone of her program, she is always in the process of reassessing the literature she chooses and her plans for incorporating books into the curriculum. She constantly reflects upon the ways in which her students talk about books and the choices she will make next. Mary sets a relaxed pace so that she, too, has the gift of time to wonder about books. She devotes a lot of time to taking stock of what books are in the collection and what directions to explore next. Good books aren't rushed; they're savored. One might see Mary cradling a child and a book in her arms—the two loves of life.

Mary's modeling of her love and enthusiasm for books is not so much conscious as it is a way of life. But because books and children are what this classroom is all about, it is easy for observers to witness this devotion to text that all the children have. Children pick up on Mary's inquisitiveness, ask questions of each other about what they are reading, and hold books dear as they would close companions. Mary and her children are truly co-producers of literary dialogue; books are the anchor points for conversation. Children are quick to realize that it is not Mary who has the answers, but *they* do as readers and responders to literature. Mary incites and provokes—all in a positive sense—a desire to be readers and hearty consumers of literature.

Building a Community of Readers

Mary expects all students to aim high—to achieve great things and to become powerful readers and writers. She knows her students well because she takes time to really listen to what they say about books. She inspires success because *all* students are considered readers and writers; everyone is a member of this club (Smith, 1988). Mary gently nudges, prods, and probes with her own statements of, "I wonder about. . . . What do you think?" "I loved this part. It made me think of a time that. . . ." "What do you think?" Her questions tapping how other members think about the books she shares aloud does, in fact, include all members of the classroom community. Every child has a voice, and all voices are valued. Mary helps to bring the richness of an aesthetic and efferent experience to literature alive for *every* student (Rosenblatt, 1938, 1978).

What is absolutely wonderful is that an observer really wouldn't be able to discriminate between the very bright students and those who are at a different place in their reading progress. All children are challenged and stretched to think in multidimensional ways.

Mary believes that it is important to reach out to the community beyond the classroom by initiating monthly "literary" happenings and other socials where family members and children come together to celebrate achievements. She casts this wider net so that families will not only understand the program but also catch the reading spirit.

Believing in the Transforming Power of Literature

Mary believes in the power of literature to transform and empower the lives of students and parents. Many children are bound by the geographic area in which they live. Children in a rural area have experiences that are, of course, different but also sometimes limited academically compared to those of more urban children. However, through books children experience the arts, different cultures, foreign lands, and journeys to fantasy worlds.

She stretches students to make connections between and among other books, illustrators, authors, and topics they've studied. Even if she may not have a connection, students sometimes come up with connections between and among books and their own life experiences she may never have imagined. Mary doesn't hesitate to pose questions she wonders about and those for which she has no answers. For Mary that is all part of being an interested and curious reader herself. She makes an effort to consciously model these kinds of questions and those which send all readers, including herself, back to the text for revisits and reconsideration.

Mary shares the ways in which books change her ways about thinking about the world. She talks about the books that have helped her grow and stretch as a reader and those she has found challenging. Her conversations with children often make connections with books she has shared with the class. Mary's interactions are authentic and don't follow any predetermined scripts. Books become the cornerstone—the building block—from which conversation blossoms and flourishes.

Inviting Reflection and Conversation About Books

Mary is forever curious about her young readers. She seeks ways to question students that invite them to reflect on how they think and feel about a book. Her questioning helps her to understand how children are reacting to text. It is a process that takes time, patience, and a perseverance to consider a text from many angles; like the turning of a kaleidoscope, the variety of conversation turns with every comment and question. Mary poses questions and statements that are invitational. Instead of always following up a child's response with "why," she also uses Chambers's (1985) recommendation, "Tell me more about how you think" (p. 173). This kind of opener leads to powerful and rich episodes of "grand conversations" (Peterson & Eeds, 1990). As one observes these exchanges, it is like friends getting together to chat about a good book, rather than the familiar classroom question/answer cycle. Instead, in this classroom, both

Mary and the children are co-producers of their own literary interpretations. Mary designs these invitations to get students to consider:

- Reactions to a book
- Why a book may be difficult or challenging to read or to listen to during read-aloud time, or why the book might have been too easy
- What connections they can make between books and their own life experiences
- A character's motivations
- The author's choice of words and illustrator's style
- A story's outcome
- What might have happened before the very first chapter of a book and what might happen after the last chapter
- Interesting and rich language
- The story from another point of view

Developing Curriculum in Response to Children's Interests

Mary follows the lead of her children in terms of curriculum planning and books to share. The agenda for talk and study emerges from shared book talk. Instead of blanketing her students with a preplanned unit or a flood of books, she thinks through the literature she will select based on the broad understandings for a unit. Then she maintains a relaxed pace to see what emerges as children talk and respond to literature. Sometimes her plans are put on hold. At other times her ideas match where students need to go next. Mary challenges and stretches students to consider new connections and more sophisticated ways of thinking and writing in response to books. Mary believes in a *balanced* perspective; she is a learner, sharer, facilitator, and coach.

Making Read-Aloud Time the Centerpiece

All of the important points discussed above are brought together throughout the day but particularly during read-aloud time. This special time is usually about an hour or so after children return from lunch. It is an extended period for Mary to interact with children over a book. This is prime time to really dig deeper into text, to savor the richness of language, and to linger over responses to questions, puzzlements, and the beauty of the total book experience.

Mary is especially perceptive to the potential of each book she chooses for this time. Borrowing Wood's (1988) term, the "literate mind," Mary, as an expert reader, is always attuned to her young novice readers. Her constant exchanges with students *during* the reading of a book (not just *after* reading the book) enable her to constantly refine her questions and pose her own puzzlements through the course of a book. Mary can't predict ahead of time where discussion over the course of reading aloud will take the group, so she relaxes into a style that is open to a myriad of possibilities. Trusting a good book to do its part, as well as allowing all to escape inside of its covers, are crucial components to Mary's style. Read-aloud times form the lasting impressions a year in this classroom has for children.

REFERENCES

Chambers, A. (1985). *Booktalk*. New York: Harper & Row.

Newkirk, T., with McLure, P. (1992). *Listening in: Children talk about books(and other things)*. Portsmouth, NH: Heinemann.

Peterson, R., & Eeds, M. (1990). *Grand conversations: Literature groups in action*. New York: Scholastic.

Rosenblatt, L. (1938). *Literature as exploration* (4th ed.). New York: Modern Language Association of America.

Rosenblatt, L. (1978). *The reader, the text, the poem: The transactional theory of the literary work*. Carbondale: Southern Illinois University Press.

Smith, F. (1988). *Understanding reading* (4th ed.). Hillsdale, NJ: Lawrence Erlbaum Associates.

Wood, D. (1988). *How children think and learn*. Cambridge, MA: Blackwell.

BIBLIOGRAPHY OF NATIVE AMERICAN LITERATURE

Accorsi, William. (1992). *My name is Pocohontas*. New York: Holiday House.

Aliki. (1976). *Corn is maize: The gift of the Indians*. New York: Harper.

American Friends Service Committee. (1989). *The Wabanakis of Maine and the Maritimes*. Bath, ME: Maine Indian Program.

Ata, Te. (1989). *Baby rattlesnake*. San Francisco: Children's Book Press.

Babcock, Barbara A., Monthan, Guy, & Monthan, Doris. (1986). *The Pueblo storyteller*. Tuscon: University of Arizona Press.

Baker, Olaf. (1981). *Where the buffaloes begin*. New York: Puffin.

Baylor, Byrd. (1974). *Everybody needs a rock*. Cedar Grove, NJ: Scribners.

Baylor, Byrd. (Ed.) (1976). *And still it is that way*. Santa Fe, NM: Trails West.

Bernard, Emery. (1993). *Spotted eagle and the black crow: A Lakota legend*. New York: Holiday House.

Bruchac, Joseph, & London, Jonathan. (1992). *Thirteen moons on turtle's back*. New York: Philomel.

Caduto, Michael J., & Bruchac, Joseph. (1988). *Keepers of the earth*. Golden, CO: Fulcrum.

Cleaver, Elizabeth. (1977). *The loon's necklace*. Toronto: Oxford University Press.

Cohlene, Terry. (1990). *Turquoise boy*. Vero Beach, FL: Rourke.

Coombs, Linda. (1992). *Powwow*. Cleveland, OH: Modern Curriculum Press.

DeArmond, Dale. (1990). *The boy who found the light: Eskimo folktales*. Boston: Little, Brown.

dePaola, Tomie. (1983). *The legend of the bluebonnet*. New York: Putnam.

dePaola, Tomie. (1988). *The legend of the Indian paintbrush*. New York: Putnam.

Driving Hawk Sneve, Virginia. (Ed.). (1989). *Dancing teepees*. New York: Holiday House.

Ekoomiak, Normee. (1988). *Arctic memories*. New York: Henry Holt.

Erdoes, Rich, & Alfonso, Ortiz. (1984). *American Indian myths and legends*. New York: Pantheon.

Erdrich, Heidi Ellen. (1993). *Maria Tallchief*. Austin, TX: Steck-Vaughn.

Esbensen, Barbara J. (1988). *The star maiden: An Ojibway tale*. Boston: Little, Brown.

Esbensen, Barbara J. (1989). *Ladder to the sky: How the gift of healing came to the Ojibway nation*. Boston: Little, Brown.

Ferris, Jeri. (1991). *Native American doctor: The story of Susan LaFlesche Picotte*. Minneapolis: Carolrhoda Books.

Fritz, Jean Craighead. (1983). *The double life of Pocohontas*. New York: Puffin.

Garaway, Margaret K. (1989). *The old hogan*. Cortez, CO: June Eck.

George, Jean Craighead. (1987). *The talking earth*. New York: HarperCollins.

Goble, Paul. (1978). *The girl who loved wild horses*. New York: Macmillan.

Goble, Paul. (1980). *The gift of the sacred dog*. New York: Bradbury.

Goble, Paul. (1984). *Buffalo woman*. New York: Aladdin.

Goble, Paul. (1990). *Dream wolf*. Scarsdale, NY: Bradbury.

Goble, Paul. (1992). *Crow chief: A Plains Indian story*. New York: Orchard.

Goble, Paul. (1992). *Love flute*. Scarsdale, NY: Bradbury.

Hausman, Gerald. (1989). *Turtle dream: Collected stories from the Hopi, Navajo, Pueblo, and Havasupai people*. Santa Fe, NM: Mariposa.

Hayes, Joe. (1988). *A heart full of turquoise: Pueblo Indian tales*. Santa Fe, NM: Mariposa.

Herbert Scott, Ann. (1972). *On mother's lap*. New York: Clarion.

Highwater, Jamake. (1981). *Moonsong lullaby*. New York: Morrow.

Highwater, Jamake. (1985). *Eyes of darkness: A novel*. New York: Lothrop, Lee & Shepard.

Highwater, Jamake. (1985). *Legend days*. New York: Harper.

Hillerman, Tony. (1991). *Hillerman country*. New York: HarperCollins.

Hirshfelder, Arlene. (1986). *Happily may I walk: American Indians and Alaska natives today*. New York: Scribners.

Hoyt-Goldsmith, Diane. (1993). *Cherokee summer*. New York: Holiday House.

Jumper, Moses, & Sonder, Ben. (1993). *Osceola: Patriot and warrior*. Austin, TX: Steck-Vaughn.

Lacapa, Michael. (1990). *The flute player: An Apache tale*. Flagstaff, AZ: Northland.

Littlechild, George. (1988). *How the mouse got brown teeth*. Saskatoon, Saskatchewan: Fifth House.

Lopez, Barry. (1990). *Crow and weasel.* San Francisco: North Point Press.

MacGill-Callahan, Sheila. (1991). *And still the turtle watched.* New York: Dial.

Martin, Rafe. (1992). *The rough-faced girl.* New York: Putnam.

Matlotki, Ekkehart. (1988). *The mouse couple: A Hopi folktale.* Flagstaff, AZ: Northland Press.

McDermott, Gerald. (1974) *Arrow to the sun: A Pueblo Indian tale.* New York: Puffin.

McLellan, Joseph. (1989). *The birth of Nanabosho.* Winnipeg, Canada: Pemmican.

Miles, Miska. (1971). *Annie and the old one.* Boston: Little, Brown.

Morgan, William. (Ed.). (1988). *Navajo coyote tales.* Santa Fe, NM: Ancient City Press.

Ortiz, Simon. (1988). *The people shall continue.* San Francisco: Children's Book Press.

Osinskil, Alice. (1988). *The Nez Perce.* Chicago: Children's Press.

Peters, Russell M. (1992). *Clambake: A Wampanoag tradition.* Minneapolis: Lerner.

Plain, Ferguson. (1989). *Eagle Feather—An honour.* Winnipeg, Canada: Pemmican.

Red Hawk, Richard. (1988). *Grandfather's origin story: The Navajo Indian beginning.* Sacramento, CA: Serra Oaks.

Rodanas, Kristina. (1991). *Dragonfly's tale.* New York: Clarion.

San Souci, Robert. (1978). *The legend of Scarface: A Blackfeet Indian tale.* New York: Doubleday.

Sewall, Marcia. (1990). *People of the breaking day.* New York: Atheneum.

Siberell, Anne. (1982). *Whale in the sky.* New York: Dutton.

Slapin, Beverly, & Seale, Doris. (Eds.). (1992). *Through Indian eyes.* Philadelphia: New Society Publishers.

Smith, MaryLou M. (1984). *Grandmother's adobe dollhouse.* Santa Fe: New Mexico Magazine.

Stein, R. Conrad. (1985). *The story of the trail of tears.* Chicago: Children's Press.

Stevens, Janet. (1993). *Coyote steals the blanket: A Ute tale.* New York: Holiday House.

Swentzell, Rina. (1992). *Children of clay, a family of Pueblo potters.* Minneapolis: Lerner.

Tanaka, Beatrice. (1991). *The chase.* New York: Crown.

Toye, William. (1979). *Fire stealer.* Toronto: Oxford University Press.

Van Laan, Nancy. (1989). *Rainbow crow.* New York: Knopf.

Viola, Herman J. (1993). *Osceola.* Austin, TX: Steck-Vaughn.

Yolen, Jane. (1990). *Sky dogs.* San Diego: Harcourt Brace Jovanovich.

About the Editors
and the Contributors

Bette Bosma is professor emerita, Calvin College, Grand Rapids, Michigan, where she taught reading and language arts for 16 years. She is the author of *Fairy Tales, Fables, Legends, and Myths: Using Folk Literature in Your Classroom*, now in its second edition, published by Teachers College Press. She conducts workshops in reading, writing, and children's literature throughout the United States and Canada.

Nancy DeVries Guth is a Calvin College alumna and the supervisor of reading and language arts for Stafford County, Virginia. She was an early childhood specialist in Brazil and an elementary and middle school teacher, as well as reading specialist, in New Mexico. Her career in Virginia began as a middle school reading specialist and supervisor of programs for elementary at-risk students. She has published a chapter in *Using Nonfiction Trade Books in the Elementary Classroom: From Ants to Zeppelins* and is co-editor of *The Greater Washington Reading Journal*.

Norma Boehm is a fifth-grade teacher and learner at Creston–Mayfield Christian School in Grand Rapids, Michigan. She also serves as a teacher consultant and researcher for the Red Cedar Writing Project at Michigan State University, supporting teachers as they develop reading/writing/learning communities in their classrooms.

Marilyn Brower taught first grade in Orlando, Florida, and Jenison, Michigan. Currently she is home with her two preschool children and tutors children in math and reading. Her love of children's literature and belief that reading is an integral part of all learning compelled her to research and field test an integrated, literature-based science curriculum.

Carole Geiger is a middle school reading specialist at Wright Middle School in Stafford County, Virginia, after a life of travels as a military wife, mother, and teacher in many interesting locations. The collaboration between Carole, the specialist, and Nancy Guth, her supervisor, was a mutually rewarding one, combining Nancy's experience with picture books and Carole's love of literature.

Mary H. Giard is a first-grade teacher at Abraham Lincoln School in Bangor, Maine. She works collaboratively with her students to integrate books across the curriculum. She presents workshops at regional and national conferences and has published in professional journals with Janice V. Kristo.

Jane Steffen Kolakowski is a teacher in a Stafford County public school and has been chosen Stafford County (Virginia) Teacher of the Year. She has a passion for all the arts in education and has published three guides for using children's books in the classroom: two for literature and language and one for mathematics and literature.

Janice V. Kristo is an Associate Professor of Education at the University of Maine, where she teaches courses in reading, language arts, and children's literature. She is particularly interested in ways teachers and children talk about books across the curriculum. Along with Amy McClure, Jan edited *Inviting Children's Responses to Literature: Guides to 57 Notable Books*, published by the National Council of Teachers of English.

Marilyn Thompson is a reading specialist at Hartwood Elementary school, Stafford County, Virginia. Her previous experience includes several years teaching second grade using themes and integrated language arts. In her current position, she provides help with the planning and implementation of developmentally appropriate thematic instruction for all levels of readers.

Index